Mastering Emotions

A Journey of Self-Discovery Towards Healing and Awakening

Salome

Mastering Emotions: A Journey of Self-Discovery Towards Healing and Awakening
By Salome
Copyright © 2020 By Salome

Self published in the USA by the author,
Contact Salome at:
MasteringEmotions@yahoo.com

ISBN: 979-8-63431-916-2
Printed in the United States of America
Book design by Robbie Adkins, www.adkinsconsult.com

Dedication

With loving appreciation
to all who contribute to my awakening
both seen and unseen
and to all who are willing to seek their inner wisdom

Special Acknowledgment

A loving thank you to my family
not quite knowing
the depth of what transpired within all these years
and loved me anyway

Table of Contents

Preface . . .

Body/Mind and Emotions are like instruments
one can learn how to play
... something realized over decades of experiencing
and learning about cause and effect of inner hurt and pain

First and foremost, I am not a doctor or psychiatrist, nor do I claim to be an authority, expert or scientist of mind, body or emotion. This book is a partial journal, one of personal experiences that led to self-discovery awakenings, realizations while living in a complex body composed of many levels and components, all interacting with each other, and one science is still exploring. This book speaks to having lived with emotional hurt and inner pain that led to insightful discoveries not only to what hurt/pain was about, but one of observing the essence of self within it. It helped me to discover how to work with and release what no longer served a purpose yet still affected my life (and still does to a lesser degree). I also came to learn I was not what my mind and emotions once led me to believe. Further explanation follows.

Being one of many pioneers on the journey of learning about hurt and pain began for me over 45 years ago. I still feel blessed having found a key that opened the door to new ideas, perspectives and a process that helped to alter my life by learning how to release stored imprints of memories still containing emotion. I won't lie. Sometimes there were many intense emotional releases I had to re-experience for moments, but once realizing I had discovered a way to release what was being felt, I became a willing participant and my journey began.

However I strongly urge anyone experiencing deep emotional pain to first seek professional assistance and not use my journey as a template. This book may offer some new insights or perspectives along the way not considered before, and perhaps some button-pressing ones as well. Just know that self-discovery is very personal and different for everyone.

Take a breath . . .

Thankfully today many new teachings and methods are available to help one understand how to release and transform those inner hurtful moments. The intention behind sharing my journey is to perhaps offer new concepts not yet known to some, or broader perspectives to those more aware of these processes. The writings are not meant to preach for these were my teachers, realizations gained after releasing emotions then writing about the experience. Some were updated from a future perspective and wisdom gained from writings long ago. The basis of the writings are discoveries made while looking within after learning how to become detached enough to observe what hurt was while experiencing it, and that messages were hidden deep within hurt or inner pain either intentionally or unintentionally placed there, unexpressed or not acknowledged. Some may carry a sense of fear to keep one from exploring, releasing it or understanding why it's there. During my experience, hurt eventually became a signpost where to look for messages to release them.

The first awareness began when observing hurt returned in cycles, and the more the signal was ignored, the more intense the pain felt each time it returned, sometimes not until months later. It wasn't until it became so intolerable, I had to pay attention and take action even though I didn't know yet what that would be. Some people are afraid to face their fears and hurts by trying to ignore, run away or find ways to mask emotions in one form or another, not feeling ready to deal with it. Mine were swallowed and not understood, without a way to express what was felt.

What many may not realize is that once the message behind hurt is acknowledged, perceived for what it is, it no longer has a reason to be carried and can be put to rest. Unfortunately many of us carry a lot of those moments, but the good news is hurt no longer has to be endured for long periods of time and can be transmuted to happier peaceful moments...in moments. New methods now teach how quickly this can be accomplished rather than falling into deep depressive states carried until one is finally able to take steps to move on or release them. I have been astounded at times of what was actually expressed behind some hurts, some revealing aha moments that left me shaking my head in awe.

Some of you may not be reading this by accident and may come to discover that will and power does exist within to literally change one's world by changing old thoughts and beliefs to new ones. This process is called Transformation, a sort of inner redecorating process. Once learning more about the process of how old beliefs and patterns are formed and carried, there are ways to master them, not be mastered by them.

I was taught that experiences are but teachers to learn from, opportunities towards building inner strength and wisdom, for how can one gain knowledge and wisdom if not knowing they may be in the midst of a lesson...judgments of them are what appears to get in the way of release instead of allowing what the lesson has to reveal as expressed, and taking action from there.

Again, the intent behind this book is to share some of what was uncovered during a very personal journey. Perhaps it may help others to look at challenge and pain a bit differently with new perspectives or perceptions. Yet please proceed with caution for some writings may possibly ignite a feeling of something within calling for your attention, and then, you also may not agree with some of what is written. If anything it may ignite or peak your curiosity enough to seek further knowledge about the subject. Just know that on a journey like this, one has to be willing to be as honest and truthful with self as one can in order to reveal, heal and release what may hurt.

NOTE: A full-on reading book this is not (by all means attempt it if you can :o)). It is more of an open-as-needed one, selecting titles from the Table of Contents that draw your attention while feeling similar emotions, or perhaps picking pages at random. These writings contain realizations or epiphanies after experiencing old emotional patterns, and writing about them had something to teach me. Perhaps some may offer a broader perspective to your experience. They are not in any particular order or linearity as emotions may rise up unexpectedly after a button pushing experience, or something that may cause one to re-experience what was deeply stored within again and again as recurring patterns. They are but signpost opportunities or calling card invitations to become aware of that which created echoes of unfinished business. When left un-attended, emotions may intensify or manifest similar emotional or physical patterns until resolved in one way or another from one's own voice and heart. There are also lighter writings that may offer glimpses into higher, happier moments that became more prevalent after releasing what no longer served.) *

You may also recognize some similar themes in several writings, or what appear to be repetitive. Some revelations have deeper layers or other aspects that offered a wider range of perception before they could be released, and some have gone very deep.

Read on . . .

Future Self Speaks . . .

Change Your Thoughts . . . Change Your World

As already mentioned, this book is about a journey of awakening compiled over a 45-year period, coming to know self by finding ways to step out of inner hurt or pain carried not understood. Back then not much existed about this subject, or even talked about, and I now surmise many just suffered in silence or managed to ignore it like I did. Am still thankful for the day a door opened for me when this journey began. It took some courage to step over the threshold to face what was not yet understood, but after reaching an intolerable level of pain, it gave me no choice. I had been given a tool and used it, then many other tools and teachings followed. After experiencing my first release from a depressive state, I saw an opportunity and became a willing participant to re-experience and observe what was being felt to discover the secrets behind what was hidden from conscious mind. At times it took courage to be truthful in facing self and cause behind some hurt and pain, but the ultimate rewards of healing for me made it worth the effort that evolved to what this book title expresses.

Content is but a partial culmination of what was discovered over many long ago moments. As I write these words in my current now moment, I can look back and reflect how far I've come as this journey still continues towards an ever-changing future. Mind you, now at age 75 am still discovering many things about the persona within that led me to this point in life. Moments of shock and awe still exist of how deeply I have been able to explore my inner world.

Finding trust, courage and willingness to reveal hurt and underlying cause gave me a process that transformed my life, especially after observing how distortions of truth and misplaced perceptions from times gone by still had a way of affecting life in ways originally not understood but ultimately led to releasing old patterns that no longer serve, mostly from unresolved past issues. Discoveries have led me to more moments of peace and happiness than ever before. You will find some writings about them as well.

While occasional pangs or twinges still exist, most are short lived, continuing to use tools and more of the wisdom gained along the way (which also appear to evolve). Admittedly once in awhile I need to be reminded not to fall back into the old-pattern feelings that still hold power within its imprinted memory, but once realized, it's sayonara in moments.

After taking the first step to acknowledge inner hurt, looking within revealed many distortions of truth and illusions they carried from what no longer existed. These were mostly from moments of trauma, unresolved issues or misconceived perceptions about self and others still carried. Allowing self to re-experience moments of old emotions helped me perceive content from new vantage points of knowledge and wisdom gained in this life since the original imprint. It allowed me to view them and life itself differently while in the process of it. Once realized, the ability to replace or transmute old thoughts and feelings with new wiser perspectives is what helped release them and more importantly forgive. Writing about what transpires often reveals what I was meant to learn from it.

Observing the effect after the very first release of hurt occurred, I felt somewhat empowered and became willing to take this journey, coming to recognize it as a way to heal and restore moments to peace. This alone at first became a motivating factor, yet honestly at times left me a bit weary, needing to take a breath or rest period before continuing. Apparently there was much to write about, far more than I could ever have imagined. Strongly felt there was intelligence behind what I was not yet aware of and it became a matter of trust to work with it, learning much later it was learning to trust of all things, a multi-dimensional me (explained further in "My Story").

Another observation revealed that while some emotional blocks were one-time memories, others had more depth than one layer (I suspect judgments of experiences along the way may have had impact, but not really sure). All I knew was that more shadow coverings (as I call them) existed also needing release. I can liken the process to restoring pieces to the jigsaw puzzle of me revealing more of the wholeness of my being.

Supportive knowledge and tools were found along the way to work with, one learning to breathe in and out of the pain while feeling the pangs of it, and not judging content if revealed.

Today many call these releases a process of re-integrating or having resolved issues be re-absorbed back into one's being, no longer having to be experienced again unless given reason. For me it was releasing many hurts, able now to fill many unloved portions within once again with love. I found that release must have meaning and intention behind it for just saying words without meaning won't always allow release until then. This is why I wait until emotional feelings begin to rise to the surface to work directly with them.

This has been a process of stepping outside of my judgmental mind to allow the experience to express itself as originally stored and imprinted within (warts and all), finding self to be worth the efforts taken. However, I found responding to a pattern the same way as before will only feed it once again to be stored away until the next opportunity arises to work with it.

Some of what was observed by my inner eye during process moments were shadow coverings of miasmic energy patterns, and when released looked like disintegrating clouds of smoke revealing a greater truth from a deeper inner knowing and intuitiveness. This also led me to discover more of who I truly am and purpose.

Often, released expressions could be a simple statement from a young child feeling hurt, a perception that formed a belief or misunderstanding from its current mind perspective as the point of origin, or an experience of trauma from elsewhere that needed to be expressed or resolved. We all have the ability within to heal – a matter of allowing it to be what it is as it appears, seeing it for what it was instead of responding to it time and again. Then comes the ability to transform it (change one's mind). And so **MASTERING EMOTIONS**, is having gained the ability to recognize them for what they are that may still affect one's life and change them, becoming the master over old perceptions and experiences instead of allowing them to be the master of one's current life and how one perceives self in it,

I have used the word "perceive" often in my writing because it has to do with allowing perspectives to be looked at differently or from a broader sense of inner vision. Some perspectives are tunnel-visioned, stuck in the time they were caught in the miasmic patterns or beliefs, stored away somewhere in body/mind waiting for a conclusion that hasn't yet occurred. Also, one may not realize that some actions taken may not be in alignment with one's true nature or self that can also cause inner conflict. A seeming unchangeable pattern can also mean one is stuck in a limited perspective of that period of time, unable to live in current times differently until forming a new relationship with it.

And there is more . . . mentioned in the Preface about the body/mind and emotions being an instrument one must learn how to play. After all this time it made sense to me. Are we not multi-dimensional beings that can also be defined by other influences within and without that affect our emotions and decision-making processes? Many are not fully aware of other components that affect body starting with how body systems work and interplay with each other. Our bodies are also intertwined with energy systems, meridians and other more refined bodies. Blockages can form from hidden underlying emotions as well as other influences. We are also composed of Chakras and as mentioned, more refined bodies all working together to create a being. One doesn't have to become an expert but at the very least becoming aware they exist can also offer wisdom on how self operates. Other aspects worth exploring are about duality, inner conflicts that can arise by not being able to make certainty decisions and listening to lower mind chatter and ego judgments that can cause confusion. Then there is DNA storage and how ancestral patterns are handed down. These are all worthy topics to explore among others for they all contribute to the process of learning how to play one's instrument, that of self, but not fully necessary in learning how to release one's emotions. I found awareness helped to more deeply comprehend the process. New horizons began to open when I sought new knowledge, and at the time also became a massage therapist for a period of time early on. I learned there was "a lot" to learn I hadn't known before about body systems as well as put me in touch with body awareness. Up to that point it was just something I thought to be part of me, not a vehicle to house all these processes. All led me to awakenings not common during that period of time, and all contributed to expanding consciousness that led to more knowledge never known before. Ever hear the expression "the more you learn the less you know". It led me places I never knew existed or ever dreamed possible…all part of another story.

The name Salome was given to me decades ago. It means peace and represented what I strived to find – stillness in peace of mind from lower mind chatter…told from stored patterns issuing fears, doubts, blame, guilt and self deprecations that maintained control over my life and beliefs…whether from me or by others. Sometimes I wondered if they were but tests of faith for how easy it sometimes is to give up and not stand up to it. It wasn't until taking back the wheel at the helm of this buggy and steer in other directions when my life began to change. And so, I began to **change my thoughts that changed my world.** While Love hasn't fully been mentioned so far, it is by far the greatest healer. Learning to fill self with love and forgiveness from my heart as old patterns were diminished and released is how I found more than enough love within to share with others.

As future self to the story that follows, the process showed me the power existing within to be able to redecorate old beliefs by replacing them with new more positive perspectives learned along the way. Prior to that I was raised in a family that didn't believe this was even possible. I found my journey had much to do with forgiving self and/or others for what was not understood, or not knowing how to respond in ways to defend self, or feel confident enough **for me to feel** "I had my back" at the time of event origin. This especially occurred when experiencing unresolved trauma, sometimes creating strings of other similar experiences that followed. I also had to forgive memories where I perceived being cause of hurt to others.

Imagine a mixture contained within perhaps lifetimes of trapped emotions, judgments, fears, distortions of truth, all fragmented and stored away until comprehending and finding methods or ways to release them and what it revealed to current self. I can now liken it all to an older computer operating system needing to be defragged.

Admittedly, through all of this I was often left with one question deep within...where is my true happy...not the kind that money or things can buy which can be momentary and fleeting. While there were and are moments of inner happy experienced from my heart, they too seem to be fleeting, but thankfully return...often. Perhaps true happiness is coming to know the power of love that exists within is stronger than what I unknowingly had allowed to have power over me. It definitely leaves me with more peace of mind than ever before, more aligned with my true purpose. Perhaps some hurt experienced was about being out of alignment with soul.

Even though knowing new challenges may be waiting in the wings that may temporarily upset my apple cart, having awareness of the process and how to work with it helps to lessen any stress involved. You might say I've become an emotional warrior by finding a way to master my inner realm, much different than being controlled by it. It became a process of transformation that continues to supply me with inner knowing and a more loving relationship with self and Creator, and more with others as well. I just take one day at a time where possible knowing more challenges may still exist, met as able to without letting judgment or self-incrimination get in the way. This is what contributes to inner strength and building a more loving attitude in my tomorrows. Did I mention the word compassion? Knowing what it feels like has tendered more compassion for others, but at times still needs work in self...and laugh at self more often lately for my foibles than I was ever able to for what used to sustain hurt.

During this journey of awakening, I also became aware of being guided and surrounded by loving beings supporting me through this journey, both seen and as part of a world not seen but felt. Not only did I begin to learn they were always there, but cherished them for having guided me to find a reconnection to my inner heart, to Source or God as I call It (the One known by many names). All helped me to begin to recognize and restore the power within that had unknowingly been given away to others while depleting self. Have also been grateful for finding others more advanced in the process of awakening who often helped me get unstuck in sticky moments, or helped me recharge during low moments until becoming more aware of the power existing within. They are all part of a support team discovered along the way, now including my inner being touching upon higher self and soul.

While this book is about what was learned about inner hurt and pain, now perceive this journey to be a lifetime process that has shifted to greater awareness of being and my place in this world, a journey I feel will continue after leaving this one. My true purpose for this life has been about tying up loose ends of unresolved issues, not only from younger years but other lifetime memories as well. This is what fed inner hurt from childhood until old enough to learn how to work with it and come to know self in a whole new light, far from the reaches of where this life began - more whole, sovereign and free than ever.

Another discovery made through my inner eye was observing a jewel, an inner diamond of many facets existing within my heart, some facets clear and shiny with many that were cloudy, covered up. As each experience was completed, another facet was cleansed allowing more and more of the beauty within the diamond shine naturally. Those moments allow more inner peace with nothing added. Even with knowing new challenges may still rise to the surface that may cause stressful moments, they are not focused on for now – hopefully you know the saying "the past is to be learned from, the future hasn't happened yet, and all that exists for now is the present" so make your present a gift for your future as much of future is created in actions of the present. As more and more people begin to recognize this, the faster the world as a whole may evolve.

However, perhaps also come to recognize that the world itself is in the process of shifting and changes affect life processes as well. Stressful situations with increased turmoil may surface faster than before. These are moments to begin to recognize and work more with inner cause/effect being pushed more rapidly to the surface and find tools or ways to reduce stress or calm down rather than react or take action from emotions that may appear. This too is a process and one that may not be easy to remember while experiencing the emotions of it. Having also learned to take one day at a time and deal with what appears in today… stuck in stress or seek peace – my choice as best as I can work with it. When peace is chosen is when synchronistic moments happen more often.

Would love to ask my even more future self where all this is leading…some day I will know when I get there and as said, just try to focus on what is presented to me in the now. Yet I must ask if my actions of today affect future-self experiences, how can I really ask that question? Many teach everything has already been done, but isn't this sort of a dichotomy to the idea of change? Sorry, can't answer that, at least not for now.

My story follows and will reveal how this journey began and where it led, yet I find a new story begins each day I open my eyes and what appears to work with, all eventually leading to gratitude for what has been shown me when current shadows dissipate.

8

To this day I continue to be thankful for that first unlocked hidden emotion revealing itself, and to all that has led me to now. I now see this journey may not have been taken had I not felt such pain of separation that led to inner discoveries, releasing me from having to ask "who am I", "what is my purpose" and "why do I hurt". While it meant coming to own up to some decisions made in lives I regretted and seeing my inner and outer worlds quite different than before, have also come to realize that apparently imperfection is truly perfection in its process that makes us who we are through the process of becoming.

On to my story . . .

My Story Simply Put? . . .

A wonderful divinely awakened teacher once taught "**Ask**, and it **shall** be given you; **seek, and ye shall find**; knock, and it **shall** be opened unto you".

There are many ways to receive in the asking and not always in the way one hopes for. It's both in the asking and willingness to receive as given, and to step through the threshold of new doors where change can begin to happen, even through inner hurt and pain.

Unfortunately, I never knew about these things until adulthood and am still in the process of discovery.

Aware of inner pain from early childhood led me to believe something was wrong with me that appeared to make me different, disconnected from others. Something felt missing that others seemed to possess in relating to each other in ways I didn't seem to have an affinity for, or could not comprehend, and judged self for and by it. No one fully discussed meanings behind feelings of love, anger, fear or inner hurt back then, sometimes only learned by observing actions taken by others, or ego-controlling situations such as being told what to do or not do, how to feel or not feel. All left me feeling very alone in my experiences, often confused about many things, and having no means or way to express what it felt like inside. Sometimes life felt like walking on eggshells with punishment if not living up to expectations of others. Sensitivity and sadness were inward activities that reflected outward. Have since learned I was far from alone in this, but here is my story.

I would often observe others laughing, playing, getting along, each seeming to connect to and share many things that went over my head, feeling apart from, not part of the group or what I observed out there. It was a very lonely existence I learned to live with and swallowed what was felt. Inner hurt led to many self-judgments and excuses by comparing self to what was observed "out there". I had no way to understand or express what I was feeling or think anyone else felt the same way. If any did they managed to hide it well or managed to express what they felt through actions taken. It also didn't help that my parents were of the "be seen and not heard" or "do as I say, not as I do" generation. After my mom became ill, it was "keep what you feel to yourself" not to upset her because stress was not good for her condition. She was already somewhat emotionally volatile because of the illness.

Feeling lost, and not quite understood, I attempted to cover it up by creating a bubble of pretense trying to be like what was observed in others (even though feelings didn't back them up), especially what I thought others expected of me, often failing to achieve it. Living this way I somehow managed to maintain a sense of connection to survive by. Sometimes the pain would disappear for awhile leaving fleeting happy moments, especially after my children were born, but along the way I observed patterns of hurt that seemed to return without rhyme or reason increasing in intensity each time. I began to liken it to being on a merry-go-round, always seeming to return to the same place once again. I wanted to get off this ride but didn't know how.

In my late twenties the patterns of returning inner hurt and pain were still not understood, yet got more intense with each return until I could no longer bear it. I still had no way of knowing why I felt it or why it existed, and the shell or bubble slowly began to disintegrate, leaving me to slowly fall apart inside, still attempting function while hiding the pain from others. Later I came to learn that swallowing or not dealing with unwanted emotions ultimately led to losing a sense of self. While living in the bubble still existing were feelings of low self-esteem, ego feelings of self doubt, inadequacies, uncertainty, being sensitive, shame, blame, as well as feelings of still not belonging or separated from – you name it, I felt it. While the created bubble managed to keep me in survival while trying so hard in many ways to fit in and belong, the bubble had no firm foundation or true substance to fill it and often failed in adulthood as I did in younger years to live up to "my" expectations. Truth was I didn't know who the real me was. As I became more aware, I realized many others who seemed to laugh and get along probably hurt inside to some degree as well, just finding better ways to cover it up differently, often through ego processes, some taking out frustrations on others weaker than themselves to increase feelings of perceived empowerment.

Being married at that time with children, I began to reach a point where I could no longer function under the false pretense of trying to be who I wasn't, not yet knowing this or how to deal with it. An inner conflict developed in trying to find answers hidden away while no longer able to sustain the façade without a stable platform. Awakening back then was in its early stages, and as I became more aware of new ideas never known before, something began to shift within. My husband didn't know how to deal with these changes as shifts took place. There had been a few moments of therapy that didn't help, drugs given me that made me feel like a zombie, and ultimately decided it was better to live with the pain and be aware of what I was going through. Needless to say, for many reasons the marriage ended as my life and pretense world continued to deteriorate. It affected my children in ways I spent years trying to make up for. There is no need to explain it all, only that I had to discover the real me that hurt, what pain covered up, and how deeply it affected my life, that of my children and others who surrounded me.

After the divorce on my own for the first time ever, I had to discover how I felt about things without outside influence and began to review life in ways already revealed. It was like going through tapes upon tapes of memories and experiences now having to decide how the real me felt about them, or perhaps rebuilding a me with new awareness, coming to perceive self and experiences in my life differently.

I began forgive what could be released while reformatting old beliefs to new ones. There had been many experiences that fed and supported old hurtful feelings in ways I was yet to learn about. I now realize at that point a lot of pain experienced was in feeling powerless and uncomfortable in my own being, not seeming able to stand up with certainty and say "this is who I am", for many times I did realize who I was not that conflicted with many life experiences surrounding me. Don't get me wrong – while I couldn't seem to deal with certain conflicts, I did seem to have a deep sense of rightness. A major question for me was asking self "why" and "what kept me from taking different actions".

Suffice to say there is no comparison or competition here that my life experiences were better or worse than anyone else experienced, or hurt more or less. A realization once showed me what hurt and pain was…just hurt and pain attached to varying levels of old stories of unresolved issues, beliefs, emotions, some stored as life patterns somewhere in mind or body. All are unique experiences according to what each of us are meant to learn from and master in life, not meant to judge self or others by. The biggest discovery about inner hurt/pain was that it intensified the longer it was ignored…if anything, just to get one's attention…and it certainly got mine.

Moving on, the door first opened in finding new ways, one to express old repressed feelings, when it was suggested to write down descriptions to what those feelings felt like – where I felt it inside, if it had dimension to it, did it have a color, did it appear to be anger, depression, etc. At the time I was feeling depressed and decided to try it. As I did this, suddenly words just poured out with pen in hand, written not from conscious thought, but flowing in expression of what was being felt. After reading what had been written, a realization followed about what depression was and why I felt it, releasing me from the feeling. Amazed, in that moment I chose not question how or where it came from but just allowed these expressions to flow freely as a process. The writings became teachers and eventually began to recognize a pattern of writing after looking within each time emotions rose to the surface. I believed them to be gifts yet very personal. It took all this time for me to be able to share them, except with a select few. What was also revealed to me was that the elevated levels of hurt and pain experienced with each return were signposts, calling card invitations to get me to pay attention and acknowledge what had once been ignored, not knowing early on how to resolve former issues carried from times of inception. And so began the process with pain as reminders when it was time to pay attention, then sit down and write. Pain diminished as I heeded its call, yet the level of hurt remained as memory had stored it.

It turned out writing about what was truthfully felt in those moments was the answer for me, for as each expression or realization was written down, the hurt diminished or disappeared according to what was learned or realized after reading what had been written, as the writings always seemed to include a lesson with it. Sometimes however, it took getting through some additional pain initiated by what was revealed, also having to be released. Through experience I learned there might be many layers or dimensional aspects to one particular lesson. However, once fully perceived, the hurt for that lesson fully disintegrated accompanied by a deep inner sigh of relief, a high I cannot find words for. It was a temporary reprieve for as I was to discover, when rested enough, the next lesson appeared that had been waiting its turn. While some harsh memories were revealed at times, the process of revelation eventually shifted becoming much easier to work with when remembering what I was doing and why.

I was also fortunate to have met a teacher when most needing one. She taught new ways of perceiving life in ways never heard about before and began to experience moments of detachment and how to observe while feeling emotions instead of fully being caught up in them. Trust with the process began to build even more. She also taught meditation and higher knowledge teachings from many cultures that shifted perceptions of life and the universe. With it inner wisdom began to emerge. This knowledge was formerly withheld by those involved in spiritual practices either because humanity wasn't ready to receive it, or by those wishing to use it to enslave others and maintain control. Besides above, we also learned what is focused on is what can become manifest like magnets to outer experiences. Apparently this is also true through collective beliefs of humanity that can manifest in the world as well. It was also learning about self responsibility to institute inner change in my life that could also affect the outer world.

Studying massage therapy was the next step. It helped to come in touch with body awareness and what was happening within it where discomfort was held and how to work with it. This opened the door to learn about healing and healing practices not aware of before. And so I began to observe what was being experienced as well as being felt in order to perceive and release what was held within with non-judgmental detachment. All this contributed towards elevating inner awareness.

The writings offered me new broader perspectives and ways to look at old beliefs differently that continued to amaze me. It also helped awaken me more to an inner world hidden from conscious awareness, and observation allowed me to view old patterns differently with something called inner vision.

An epiphany one day showed me I was able to view old patterns stored in the body not only with fresh new eyes from knowledge and tools picked up along the journey, but also able to change patterns as they rose to the surface and were experienced. This was an introduction to transformation or transmuting miasmic energy patterns. Inner vision revealed distortions of truth or perspectives stored from other times. The new teachings not only revealed the old patterns differently, but allowed me to at the time of perception, change the pattern to something more loving and current, then write about them from new perspectives of what had been learned as a result. I think I had already been doing this to some degree, but this new awareness allowed me to become more of a conscious participant in the process.

Over the years practicing observation to master emotions instead of being an effect of them was also learning how not to judge or respond to what was expressed and felt about self or others as content revealed itself. These old patterns could contain strong feelings still attached to old memories that no longer served a purpose but were still trapped. During the processes of release and learning how to transmute old energy patterns to new more positive ones, compassion began to form when observing others hurting realizing they too had stories of inner hurt.

I also began to observe that many experiences out there are but mirrors to what exists within. Often if the mirror reflected hurt or pain inside, perhaps by someone pressing some buttons, it usually meant something inside needed to be addressed and resolved in what was reflected. The mirror became another signpost or indicator of something that could be healed from within, changing out there. The mirror also revealed that often some people have a tendency to place blame for their pain on others when emotions are activated, not yet realizing it is a reflection to something in self that may need attention. Yet, could the one being hurt also be a mirror to the person seeming to cause the hurt. Once reflected upon, the experiences of victimhood can begin to change after new perceptions and perspectives are formed. Have become even more aware that within is an innate sense of what feels right when all is in alignment with our higher self and soul purpose, and hurts can also be signposts leading to areas when not aligned. Remember my saying I couldn't relate to the laughter observed in childhood that hurt within? Those pictures also gave me an inkling of how life could become but too much stood in my way to reach the observed happiness. By discovering and transmuting inner blocks, I began to experience more moments of happiness without cause or reason, and yes, a journey still in progress.

The difference is many of my generation were not taught much of this growing up for parents most likely taught us based on the limitation factors of how they were raised, as I taught my children from those limiting experiences as well. The good news is everyone has the ability and power to change what has been limiting by coming to understand where blocks and limitations exist and what put them there, then develop a process and find tools to change and create new happy from. This knowledge does exist but has been kept (even today) hidden from many for purpose of control, some using it by instigating us to place blame for our feelings on others for what we feel inside, or make others feel they are not worthy or lesser for it to salve their own ego. All are experiences to learn by, not suffer for.

Thankfully reawakening is happening in our world and many are beginning to reclaim their power once unknowingly (or knowingly) given away to others. To me this has also been a process of becoming enlightened (by releasing burdens no longer needing to be carried). How far this journey goes is yet to be discovered.

Each of us can begin to recognize and see the fear bred and fed in us as illusory beliefs to feed ego mind (some call monkey mind) that can be resolved, dissolved and replaced with more positive outcomes. Also thankfully today many tools and knowledge exists to assist the process humanity is awakening to. We all have a right to be and exist in wholeness, sovereignty and freedom. Once coming to perceive that inner fear is but an illusion, coverings formed to keep us from recognizing and taking steps towards regaining what is meant to be ours, we all may become aware of the oneness of us many don't yet perceive.

Have been slowly discovering that my story has not only been about learning what it has to teach in uncovering, but the ultimate truth for me was realizing that no one could give me what I truly felt was wanted or needed but self, and have been learning to fill my cup to share with others rather than trying to get it filled by others.

Another lesson was that to abuse power to control others is to create more darkness within self that eventually will have to be dealt with...perhaps not in this life but many to come.

And lastly, the darkness within is but a shadow of the true self, not one to be feared but understood and worked with. Too many have been taught to be fearful and angry among dysfunctional emotions to keep from discovering the power within. How many have actually noticed that more and more digital items and programs on TV and movies, games of destruction, and social media keep our focus more on the outer world, reporting more about chaos to keep people emotionally responsive to maintain what is detrimental to creating peace and harmony and keep many from focusing within where all can begin to heal?

While learning to discern and observe feelings in the midst of experiencing them, many tools have been acquired along the way to support my journey. One important one is learning to focus on breathing through the experience. Others use tapping or repeating positive powerful statements or affirmations, changing the thought process or finding other ways to achieve transmuting the miasmic energy patterns they are aware of. I was also taught that what we do today creates our future, and bringing about a positive change can create a more positive future, not only for self but others as well. This information has given me renewed strength and impetus to keep this journey going.

I used to blame self deeply for making mistakes but now they are part of the learning process that provides wisdom. The best part for me is achieving more and more moments of stillness, a "no thought" process called Being. Look up the title "Being" in the Table of Contents which expresses what I feel being present in moments of full awareness, allowing self to just Be with nothing added. In those moments there is no control or judgment just pure awareness, inner peace and knowing. One day I hope to live like this in all moments.

All of this led me to fully realize that this is a journey only I could take for no one else could do it for me, and I do have the power to change my life and not leave the job up to others. At an earlier stage of life I had sat at the foot of many mountains in fear of failure until I had the courage and willingness to begin to climb, coming to know failures are part of the learning process leading to wisdom, problem solving and building strength of character through belief in self, even by wading through all the experiences of hurt and grief with buckets of tears – sometimes taking two steps backwards for one step forward. How many more exist I do not know as each experience is different. It's up to me to find the willingness to meet each challenge faced to learn how to master each one as described above. I also had to recognize any fear behind what seemed to hold me back from taking the next step... and not beat self up if it wasn't accomplished in that moment – all valuable lessons in learning to trust self above all through the power of source that exists within – the One that gave me the gift of life I had to learn how to appreciate and cherish.

And so I leave you with this thought – your story is unique as well, so . . .

On to Your Story . . .

The cause of inner hurt and pain in my story and what experiences led to them is really irrelevant. Your story of hurt and pain is quite different than mine, but doesn't mean any more or less hurt was felt by any degree until able to find release. Discoveries are not meant to judge or place blame on who, what, where or when, but more importantly to recognize cause of hidden inner issues connected to what is being felt and find ways to change and release old energy patterns to new more positive ones.

One person may erroneously think there are inner demons to face within, not knowing the old feeling and belief only exists because they were knowingly or unknowingly embedded somewhere within waiting to be recognized for what they are and released as described above. Often the missing ingredient is not feeling loved by others, and by self. How can one expect others to reflect what isn't felt inside?

Repetitive negative reactions or response mechanisms to such experiences is what appeared to keep them alive. Perhaps they became more expansive by accumulating distortions along the way, that which may have been created in another time period carried over to a time one may have more awareness and knowledge how to restructure and release what one didn't have the ability to do before, but may have now.

Based on what observation taught me about pain, some may want to run, take drugs to cover fear and pain or perhaps need to take more drugs when hurt reappears, even to the point of taking one's life. Again what may not be understood is inner hurt and pain are but messengers to get one's attention. The more one may run, the more intense the pain may become until ready to deal with it. Facing self at times may be fearful, but ultimately a freeing experience,

While feeling low enough at times there was thought towards taking my life, I knew it wasn't an option because some of the suffering was carried over from a time when I did commit suicide. I came into this life to heal what I could because I thought taking my life in that life would resolve what caused me to run. Sorry folks, I'm here now to take care of what couldn't be resolved before and knowing repeating actions would only delay the inevitable. If feeling that low, there is a title about suicide and what I had to learn in how to value and cherish life instead. Truly hope all can find ways to re-discover and restore their inner peace and the power within that is already yours.

This book doesn't have an ending ... Beyond this point becomes "Your Story" among the many other stories that exist within this paradigm. Life is constantly changing and with it so are we. Hopefully many realize after grasping what this book has been about, by staying stuck in old ways is what keeps them there.

If any of this resonates with you, may the inner hurt and pain of your story show you the way towards providing fruits of wisdom, clarity and peace of mind, heart and soul. May each reader find their own expressions and discoveries leading towards releasing what no longer serves and find those moments of truth that blossom to light ... your way ... and let it carry you safely to discover how to free yourself from that which may bind and limit you so the facets of your inner diamond reflects the light you truly are meant to be shining brightly from the light within.

Prologue . . .

Here is a sharing of some things observed and learned along the way:

These are not judgments but emotional feelings that have risen or became manifest observed to learn from, old patterns attached to memories of unresolved issues or experiences of trauma and beliefs about self – recognizing some signs that may have led to cause behind hurt or pain:

- ☀ Illusions of an emotional mind, is definitely not time to make decisions or take responsive actions to until calm is restored

- ☀ Deep depression may stem from not receiving what is wanted or not being able to control a situation

- ☀ Unexpressed emotions and unresolved issues – ignoring what is being felt and internalizing

- ☀ Insecurity in not feeling worthy enough

- ☀ Fearful of the strength of pain in not knowing its cause, or not feeling strong enough to handle or master what is felt

- ☀ Belief in lack of ability or something is wrong with self

- ☀ Feeling shame, blame and other emotions

- ☀ Not feeling love for self and lacking self respect

- ☀ Self punishment for seemingly unable to do or accomplish what is wanted

- ☀ Inability to take control of situation

- ☀ Too much negative emotional response or reactions that keep attracting similar experiences until creating change

- ☀ Putting off taking action not knowing what to do or how to resolve

- ☀ Not wanting to deal with pain or take responsibility for cause of it – running away in fear

- ☀ Remorseful thinking of other ways situations could have been handled by repeating emotions that keep them active
- ☀ Forming judgments of what is revealed
- ☀ Experiencing dichotomy of being told how to feel vs. what is actually felt that creates inner conflict
- ☀ The duality of waffling back and forth, not yet able to make a firm decision about something causing confusion or conflict
- ☀ Discovering that some experiences may have many layers and facets connected to it

Lessons learned by working with and through hurt and pain:

- ☀ As a tool, willingness to step beyond fear without judgment is to observe and allow full expression in order to release what is being shown. If you've ever experienced Shiatsu where a pain felt is pressed into, it will hurt more for a moment but soon the congestion of it will release – it's something like that.
- ☀ How to work with healing is beginning to recognize that healing is an inside job
- ☀ If fearful at first, take baby steps. Courage will follow after coming to recognize distortions of truth from other periods of time no longer serves a purpose except to educate and be free from carrying it again
- ☀ Asking self to reveal unexpressed content to conscious awareness is a good first step
- ☀ Acceptance and courage to face truth in self is the most freeing experience – avoidance in fear is what keeps hurt active
- ☀ Freedom to make other more positive choices from wisdom learned
- ☀ Taking responsibility by responding in positive ways to what is revealed is to be in partnership with the healing process
- ☀ Able to look at similar experiences in different ways

- Allowing emotional expressions to flow without judgment is allowing old miasmic patterns to be revealed without getting mind involved or caught back in the emotion. Once expressed, it is a revelation and opportunity to change old perceptions to more positive ones that support happiness. Judgment will keep them active until being willing to let them go

- Tears and crying are cleansing – even if not knowing why (mine were buckets). Still happens occasionally but smile more often.

- Learning to ask for divine help, guidance and support instead of belief in having to continue to suffer. One can also ask to go through experiences with ease and grace.

- Coming in touch more and more with one's inner light and wisdom, and what one is meant to learn and accomplish in this life (not being sidetracked by shadow distortions)

- One pattern may have many strings connected to similar experience(s) in this and other lives, more than one facet to the same lesson

- With release, change in attitude and perception happens naturally

- Wisdom comes from looking at experience differently

- Forgiveness of others and, more importantly, self

- Learning to love self begets more love in gifting to others and one can only give from what they already have

- Building a new and more loving and respectful relationship with self is what begins to manifest out there

- More self assurance and self worth is gained from loving self

- More appreciation, compassion and less judgment resolves issues faster

- It's been said time and again over millennia that love and forgiveness heals all internal wounds and others as well

- What is released and transformed from within is what allows more loving ways to become manifest outwards

✻ Ability to see the gifts one has been given and be thankful for them

✻ Learning to listen more intently to the intuitive part of self

✻ Being blocked from taking certain actions or directions can also mean being kept safe from heading in a direction not meant to be taken, and if taken may have other lessons to learn. When in alignment with higher being, all falls into place with ease and grace

✻ Observing that making mistakes can help one learn from them offering wisdom from the lesson, not incessantly to be punished for

✻ Giving up trying to control allows what is meant to be to flow more easily

✻ One person's perceived weaknesses CAN become their greatest strengths and one's perceived enemy can become their greatest ally

✻ Increase knowledge and wisdom by being more open to listen to other(s) ideas and ways of their perceived truth can broaden one's horizons. Each apparently holds a unique piece to the whole of the story being played out, and how one responds is really an indication of something going on within self

Infinite blessings of love and light to all!

Acceptance

First
acceptance
then
understanding
That's the rule
towards learning
truth

Truth becomes knowing
perceiving
an integral part of one's inner being
An unfoldment of the soul

It is much like a rose
Each petal unfolds perfectly
releasing the light of inner beauty
but unlike a rose
the soul continues to shine

It is not a matter of belief
To accept is to acknowledge
an existence of possibility not yet known
a way perhaps not visible to the naked eye
requiring proof
until coming to know it
within one's soul

From acceptance
comes perceiving
a form of understanding

From understanding
comes inner truth
a knowing of rightness

What follows is wisdom
gleaned from acceptance of possibility
where truth has led
to knowing

Then one stands stronger
as part of a greater whole

Accepting Self

After a lifetime
of sorting through emotions
sifting through an ocean
of hurt and pain
from mixed messages
gleaned from looking out there
in trying to fill in empty spaces
of not knowing who I am
or meant to be
often not relating to others
while attempting to find
seeming missing pieces of self
I finally found
my own voice

How wonderful that feels

In coming to know my own mind
I can relate to the fullness
of who I truly am
and no longer need to try
to fit into other molds
of not being tolerated
or looked down up
for being different

I know now
that out there
couldn't relate to me
as I could not to them
while I tried to figure out
and observe
who I was in this world

By learning how to accept self
by seeing more clearly
through my own eyes
I now feel more beautifully comfortable
in my own skin
of being who I am
in my surroundings among others

The lesson learned is
how can I possibly expect others
to accept me
If I couldn't accept self first

And if another doesn't feel comfortable
being around me
or cannot be accepting of me as I truly am
I now know it's something needing to be looked at
perhaps within each of us
to find out why
as I did for myself

Acknowledgment

I've unconsciously sought acknowledgment
from others
to know I'm loved
to know I've done the right thing
to know my abilities are worthy
mainly out of uncertainty
much as a child who never grew up
not wishing to take responsibility for failing to have certain
    qualities
to be the image I wish to be
needing someone else to tell me
"you're alright, you're okay"
not seeming to know it for myself
and hurting
if someone did not agree

In letting go of fears, doubts and negative beliefs
being willing to take responsibility for my actions
I've discovered new feelings coming from within
More of a refined guidance
a voice that can only be heard
when all my ego mind's thoughts and ideas
have been quieted
able to hear within
the One that is true acknowledgment
the true image
the Source of all that is within

The One contains all the qualities
I did not believe were there
and can only be reached when willing
to give up the idea that something is missing

An Emotional Battlefield –
Victory At Last

You name it
I've experienced it
the highs and lows of emotion

For some reason I've been given
the gift of words to express what is felt
along with the ability to observe while feeling it
at the very same time

At first I was a survivor
living with hurtful emotions that didn't have a name
or expression
then the door opened
and here I am later in life
still releasing them
not as an effect of them
but with purpose in acceptance of cause

I have seen how patterns of my life
affected my actions
old beliefs that got in my way of living life
memories that carried hurt
unresolved issues of the past
and recognizing other life experiences that created them

It has been a long journey and I am victorious
for while emotions still exist
I live peacefully in many more moments than before
From time to time some may want to draw me back into the storm
I now see them as old memory patterns rising to the surface
ones that no longer serve a purpose but can leave me with wisdom

I am able to quickly master cause and effect and affect a
    release
even if it takes more than a moment
for I've learned to observe what it has to teach
willing to listen to and acknowledge its message
perceive truth behind the veil of shadow and move on

Once an old memory of hurt serves its purpose in getting my
    attention
it no longer has a need to exist

Anger - Fear - Love

I've confronted and explored
the face of anger
It is a dark place
void
empty of all true feeling
except anger
It's not a pleasant place to be in
There is no love
because it is waiting to be filled with love

I've confronted and explored the face of fear
It too is devoid of true feeling
an empty space that needs to be filled
and fear of not knowing why was very hard

What is fear
but not trusting
and what is anger
but not loving

I've been afraid more
when I've not seen love within me
I've been angry only because
I have not been able to love

The good news is
as soon as love replaces
the emptiness that was filled with fear or anger
(be it in thought or feeling)
the anger or the fear goes away

Transformation takes place

and love
which is the only true feeling
is restored to its rightful place
that which brings wholeness and healing

One may consider empty space
a multi-dimensional easel
Since we are all artists
we all have control of the brush
and if the colors of fear or anger
have filled the empty space
guess who painted it
and guess who can change it

I admit it once was not easy at all to do this
but as a true artist learning his trade
each brush stroke gets easier
each attempt at mastering the art
gets stronger
until the true masterpiece is created

My masterpiece is not yet completed
but at least I know
(with relief in my heart)
that I am in the process of creating it

Apathy

Don't pity the man who sees and hears
but does not have a way to speak his mind
for he has courage and knows what he can do
beyond his handicap

Pity more the healthy man
who speaks his mind
but cannot see or hear
beyond his own apathy

Asking

I felt good today
I had thanked Creator
and all the unseen forces around me
for providing healing to my soul
when I asked

I grew up never knowing
that I could

When I did ask today
suddenly out of nowhere
in my mind's eye
sparkles of glittering lights
of many different colors
descended upon me
surrounding me like twinkling particles
made of beautiful and brilliant colors

I became giddy
filled with laughter
lightness of being
beyond description

 I wanted to share the joy
and sent the glitter
out into this world
letting these beautiful sparkles
descend upon the whole earth
praying that all upon the earth
also feel the love
and lightness of being

It didn't last a long time
but I was reminded of what it feels like

to feel happiness for no other reason

This feeling was a gift
one I should remember to ask for more often
especially if I'm feeling down

Awakening

Every step I take
leads me to the next

And as I walk this path
one step at a time
one truth at a time
I find freedom
from being who I thought I was
to becoming
Who I am

Balance

Experiences are about
learning to find balance
living at times in extremes
of one side
or the other

This is a process of learning
that helps one find the middle road
of balance between the two
achieved when one has finished learning
what it felt like
to live the extremes of both sides

With the middle road comes inner peace
allowing the mind to see clearly
and the true heart to flow freely

Balance - Pathway to Peace

I've heard it said
we experience opposites to learn from each one

Light and darkness
are two sides to the same coin
as up is to down
love is to hate
and any other opposition
for how would one know what each side feels like
without having experienced the other

Living in extremes of either side
can cause imbalance
ignoring one side over the other

Isn't it better to walk in the middle
standing in the center of both
knowing the difference between the two
to bring about a third state of balance and peace
the home of unconditional love

Living balanced is also the core of one's
Inner strength and peace

Staying there is another matter
but one can always return when ready

Being

Words cannot fully describe Being
It's an awareness, an inner knowing, a state of allowing
whatever is to Be whatever is
without attaching anything to or reacting to it
With Being all flows freely in synchronicity
an experience of emotions without attachment to absolute joy
　　or sorrow
one is all things in a state of balance
of well being
It is being fully present in experiencing the moment of now
not yesterday or tomorrow

Mind is at peace, away from controlling emotions
without thoughts of why you are feeling
what you are feeling
What and why no longer are part of one's vocabulary
for the answers become known
because you allow them

There is no need for mundane thought
to judge experiences
based on concepts of yesterday
There is no need to place thought in tomorrow
for that too is based on concepts of yesterday
and you would only end up repeating
yesterday in tomorrow

The activity of the mind is completely at rest
in experiencing the moment of now
All is seen and heard with inner senses instead of ego mind
for they have been cleared from being lost among thought
You are in touch with that which you are
not what thought has conceived you to be
awareness intensifies

abilities multiply
Much can be accomplished for there is no longer a belief in
    can't
you know you can
and do
because thought was not placed on whether you could or not

Love is unconditional
life is full from moment to moment
Life is

BEING

Being Held Back Can Be Magic

Sometimes magic happens
in the most unexpected ways
in moments that don't appear
to give one what is wanted

Perhaps one may feel the frustration
of being held back
from going in a specific direction
or from reaching a goal
unable to accomplish what is wanted
after attempting to make it happen
over and over again

I've experienced many like moments in my life
and yet
now realize that if I hadn't
my path may have taken different directions
for better or worse
I cannot say

What I do know now is
I wouldn't have come to know what I learned
or reached the level and depth of understanding or knowing
    given to me

And very often
what was received in its place was even better
than what I could have imagined or hoped for

I've watched paths being blocked many times
in ways I would have wanted to go
and when it felt something like a salmon struggling to get upstream
the fight was given up knowing in my heart

a new direction had to be taken

Many times I learned in taking new directions
when doors opened easily
and everything fell into place
like magic
it was then I knew
I was where I needed to be

Can someone tell me we are not directed
to be in the right place at the right time

It only takes a moment to get the message
if something is not working right
to try something different
and let the magic happen

Belief

If one must argue with another
over a belief in ideals
then perhaps
one does not really believe in his ideal at all

It is much better to live your ideal
and set an example
rather than trying to convince yourself
by arguing the point

Building a Life

During parts of my life
I have walked through it
much like an architect or engineer
following a schematic for living
but not being at the heart of it
at times, not enjoying the journey
not loving the design
or not feeling part of it
just following the path of how I felt it should become
through mind without heart and soul

What I hadn't realized
was that these were blueprints
steps towards reaching my true heart
by doing what I intuitively knew was right
even when I didn't feel it

And if I rebelled and refused to follow the plan
by wanting to use methods more to my liking
it took me on paths that delayed the construction schedule
yet teaching me much along the way
always seeming to return time and again to continue
with the master plan

I have been building a foundation
with that blueprint without knowing
or quite understanding what the plans were
until they unfolded before me
Yet I know somewhere within me
I am the engineer, builder and creator
providing each part of the plan
with tools for which to build the structure
I've come to see as standing strongly and firmly
upon the foundation

with universal love as its mortar
and with soul as my guide
to complete the plan or purpose of my life
as it was meant to be

Challenges of Life

How did things come to be so difficult

I was told my source is
lightness of being
and yet life for me has been a struggle

At times I've sat at the foot of the mountain
lamenting the climb
and other times I've experienced the exhilaration
of reaching the top
only to slide a bit backwards
or to find another mountain
in the midst of my exhilaration

I have my moments
of joy
of clarity
lightness of being
and I want to know why it's been such a struggle
to get here
and why I make it so

I only ask because at times I still struggle
and the only one who can answer this
is me

It is quite different than the first time I became aware
By looking back to the beginning of this journey
through awareness
I see myself in quite another place
definitely lighter of being than ever before
and far more knowledgeable
equipped with all the tools I may ever need (or not)

I have met many mountains
and eventually climbed them all
but once in awhile
I still end up sitting at the foot of one
one that looms large before me
and wonder as I do now
why it seems so hard for me to want to climb this one

I can only thank God at the moment
for coming to know
that obstacles are not the true reality
but are challenges that can be met
one way or another

Right now I may not feel like meeting it
but at least I can take heart that it will happen at some point

Writing these words have been a catharsis for me
a way to express what I feel
to step back for a moment and look
at what I'm truly feeling
where I've been
where I've come to
and where I'm going

Just by writing what I've felt right now
has changed it
given it a new dimension for me to look at

I'm human
with days that are more challenging than others
Sometimes I can easily find the ways to meet them
and other days I don't want to go another step

What I am realizing now is

that it's okay to rest for a moment without guilt
knowing that it is not because I'm lost or a victim of
     circumstance
or unable to meet a challenge
or that I can't

I know I will when I'm ready
and it's great to realize I have that choice

Challenges of Life Met

I've crossed another line of challenge so to speak
so thankful to be where I am right now
looking back at instead of towards

Being on this side of the line is powerful
It says "I've conquered" what was placed before me
and as my reward
this side shows me the wisdom of the ages
as well as feeling a wonderful sense of freedom
where just moments ago I cowered
on the other side of its shadow

Ignorance and abjuration is what kept me there
Determination is what brought me here

Now I can continue my journey
…until the next challenge appears

Change It !

I look deep inside
and what do I see
what irks me out there
is really in me

And what I love most
comes deep from the heart
which is used to forgive
this non-loving part

Inside is the place
to look and make change
not something out there
you want rearranged

The very first step
is to love what is there
no matter how hard
or deep it appears

It may reflect anger
contempt or disgust
esteem that is low
or a flash of mistrust

And then comes forgiveness
for what had been done
It really was me
that triggered the gun

It mirrored my feelings
to show me the way
the choice was then mine
that it go or it stay

No matter the cause
no matter the name
the object is "change it"
not make more of the same

And much like some magic
the change will occur
perhaps not right now
or in ways I'd prefer

And last but not least
bless "who" played the part
the one that had helped
to make this change start

Because of that "one"
I'm now totally free
of a part that was hidden
that held misery

Changing Focus

As I grew up, those in the world taught me to focus on

- what was not good and ugly in the world
- what was to be feared
- what was missing in my life
- what were not my best traits, what was wrong with me and to feel bad about them
- what to be wary and afraid of
- what you can't, not can or why
- how to be cautious and careful by believing in limitations in one's thinking and doing
- that making mistakes was a terrible thing

taught to me by those who had been taught these things as they grew up and as I so taught my own children. But somehow I also learned and left them with qualities of honesty, truth and goodness and an ability to find their own way,

As I grew older and could now think for myself, a new teaching and way to focus was taught to me

- to look beyond what I think and feel for what is seen isn't always the whole picture
- to look upon the beauty in and of the world, for it also exists
- to look upon and be thankful for what I have, not what I don't
- to focus more on love than fear
- to focus more on light, not darkness and learn what darkness had to teach
- to see the wonderful things I am, not what seems to be missing or wrong, for they too are learning experiences
- to be thankful and celebrate, not lament
- to allow the sun to shine upon my being, not the shadows, for fear is only a shadow and not reality
- that mistakes made are only learning experiences

✻ that one's truth exists as far as one allows themselves to
   perceive it

Changing focus - - it sounds so easy
but sometimes I struggle just to remember
for the old way is a habit pattern seemingly deeply embedded
sometimes not easily changed

But as I become more aware of it
it gets somewhat easier and easier as I learn and discover
that when one focuses on the darkness and what isn't
that's what they will continue to see and bring to themselves
and
when one focuses on the light and what is
that's what they will see and bring to themselves

It is becoming more apparent to me that it is a choice
and were we not given choice as a gift - -

The rub is that it is up to us to learn how to use it - -
and as more and more people make the "light" choice
towards our highest good
more of darkness or shadows will begin to fade into oblivion

A quote from Somerset Maugham is now one of my favorites:
"If you refuse to think or accept anything but the best,
it is true that very often in your life you will get it"

Choice

We always have choice
In the decisions we make

Some are harder to make than others
they are made moment to moment
go left or right
eat or not
hurt or love
anger or forgiveness
go safely or take a risk
greed or good intention
are but a few

But there are harder choices in life
Does one go with ego desire
or what is known to be better for us

Sometimes one does not hear their inner voice
the quiet one within
that tells us the best choice to make
for our highest good

Call it conscious awareness
Intuition, guidance or inspiration
it exists in all of us
and the choice is always
whether or not we choose to listen

Ego and desire may not always agree
with the wisest choice to make
but the outcome of listening to the inner voice
will provide the richest experience
beyond its weight in gold

But even when choosing unwisely
this choice will also provide something to learn
an opportunity to perhaps to learn through a harsher
    experience
a struggle that may delay reaching the better choice
yet leaves a trail towards truth and wisdom

This choice may lead one on a tougher road
with a harder lesson to learn
and perhaps still get to where you needed to go in the first
    place
It just may take longer to get there

The point is
we always have choice
and what a gift it is

Completion

In the ways of the world
I've been but a weary traveler
seeking truth
searching for clues to my identity
finding yet another piece to the puzzle
rejecting and accepting
until more of the pieces come together

The body carries me through the experience
the mind is an observer
the light is my guidance
and my heart renders the decision
until each piece fits perfectly

Control

One may not be able
to control the experiences happening in one's life
But one can control how they respond to them
and that alone
will bring about change

Controlling Emotions

I've built a dam inside
one to control the flow of the emotions
of love and giving
to protect my vulnerability

I've found that I've opened the locks
more to some than others
sometimes shutting the locks for protection
to keep myself dry, cold and unfeeling
Other times the flow is great
and shower others with all I have to give

When I stop the flow I am but a shadow of truth
pretending to be the real thing
living the way I think it should be
and not the way it is
trying to control to make things happen my way

Fear is greater because I am unsure and feeling alone
there is an emptiness inside
and I feel blocked in holding back

It's times like these
I only give the small amount that's there to give
depending on if I feel it's deserving

I've controlled the flow living defensively
more out of reaction to others and to life
to protect my vulnerabilities
unsure of who I am and what I'm capable of
not fully realizing
that I have been the keeper of the locks
that I alone have kept my valleys dry and infertile
by feeding fears, doubts and negatives

When I totally allow the flow to freely come through
I am all things
the reality, not the shadow
There is abundance to give to all
without thought of who is deserving of it

I am fulfilled and whole
knowing and protected
because the flow is that which comes from Source
that which I call God

Courage

It takes courage for one to face self
only to find out underneath it all
one is not what or who
they believe themselves to be

It was worth the journey to take the risk
to find the real me

Creation Through the Microcosm

What I've observed is
the lower mind is but a shadow of the higher mind
We are meant to create from higher mind ideals
not through base emotions of the lower one
The higher mind is a gift given to us
with unlimited resources
limited only according to lower mind beliefs

Perhaps the lower mind is there to teach
how to use the higher mind power
learning how to consciously manifest happiness
instead of suffering
for are we not children of the Creator

Emotions and beliefs born from shadow
may become manifest
perhaps as an opportunity
to see our creation of limitation
an opportunity to deem
whether we like our creation or not
and what repercussions may occur
by actions taken

One can fall deep into the pit of darkness
of lower mind experiences within shadow
an empty space devoid of love and light
sometimes appearing as a deep endless pit
of emotional turmoil
not fully realizing higher mind
is where power given us is limitless
true power connected to Creator within us
through love and light of the higher mind heart
meant to foster happiness within self

and share our bounty with others
What appears through lower mind
are distortions of truth
selfish ego driven facets of personality
formed through shadow not from light
a shadow fed through reactive base emotions
of lower mind ego
those fleeting moments of satisfaction
not sustainable
filled with disappointments and sadness
always seeking fulfillment never found

When seeking to manifest
our deepest heart desires through higher mind
it would become manifest through a heart
meant to experience joy, love and light
inner truth, wisdom and happiness
higher mind ideals
from an unlimited supply of resources

So which mind
would one choose to manifest from
if given the choice

The choice is ours
and always has been

Dance With Life

Like a leaf that flutters in the wind
Like a tree that sways to the song of the breeze
Like the rhythm of two bodies moving joyfully in the night
Like the child soaring high on a swing neath the trees
This is the dance of life

Let the spirit of life move you to and fro
Let the music of the heart twirl you around
Let your soul be lifted to lofty heights
While your feet meld firmly with the ground

Rush with the tide flowing in and out
Feel the wind as it caresses your face
Learn what those fears and doubts are about
Bring yourself to a loftier place

Move to the song on the radio
Learn the beat of your own inner drum
Hear all that is the music of life
And let the movement freely come

Open your heart to the beauty of dawn
Cleanse yourself with the freshness of dew
Feel the power of light caress your soul
Learn to flow with all that is true

Feel the joy of love in your heart
Smile from within and let yourself heal
Chase away darker clouds that appear
Imbue the self with all that is real

Dance with life

Darkness – Friend or Foe

We are of the light
and darkness seems to be a teacher
Darkness falls within the category of shadow
the one represented by lower mind
It appears whenever a path or action chosen
is less than loving

It can be as deep as it needs to be
a seeming endless pit
a very lonely place
a void of fear
anger
or anything that is not loving

It can engulf us
as long as it is needed to be there
as long as it takes for us to learn from it

It appears as an enemy
something to be resisted
But we give it an invitation
through some of our actions
that create darkness
in thought and emotion
and through judgment calls
we may make upon others and ourselves
that are less than loving acts

And then when it appears
sometimes we run from it
or sit quietly in its wake
motionless or suffering
from the pain we allow it to cause
sometimes debilitated

and unable to function because of it
until its passing

Some fear this darkness
Some judge it and themselves by it
Some operate from and through it
using it at times against others to seek release
Some use it to abuse to make themselves feel better
or are abused by it

The depth of darkness within shadow
is our creation
We invite it in
We feed it
We maintain it
We embellish it
Many learn to live within it
and through it
sustaining it as long as it is needed
or until coming to understand its nature
and why it's there

It is not real
It contains distortions of truth
a voice we may choose to listen to
from and through the lower mind
It can taunt and tantalize
drawing us through our basest emotions

It can give rise
to feelings of self righteousness
not self rightness

Darkness can be termed negativity
a cloud that covers the ability
to have clarity of mind

to see the truth through wisdom
of the heart
from the essence of
our soul and being

So what is the essence of darkness?
Why does it exist
Where does it come from
What is its purpose
What gives rise to it
And why are we afraid of it

Could it be there to teach us
something that we don't yet understand
or cannot yet see
about ourselves

It comes and goes
not always by invitation

It expresses itself as loudly as we need it to
to make us listen and pay attention
in order to learn what it is teaching us
about ourselves
trying to get our attention to take a good look
at the essence of what encompasses
the truth it has teach

If one can learn to step back
and observe the hurt being felt
with courage instead of fear or judgment
no matter how harsh it may appear to be
If one can make the choice
to listen and perhaps allow self
to face the fear of self
to experience the feeling one more time

with enough detachment to observe
to perceive the essence of truth behind it
it will have served its purpose
and then dissipate
because of willingness to hear its message

Tears may flow
sometimes in buckets
but they are healing waters
washing away all the debris no longer needed

Darkness can be a lonely hurtful place
but a place one doesn't
have to live in for very long
It is always our choice
to listen, learn and let go
or to perpetuate it
And when we choose to listen
it will leave us with a greater sense of self
and more moments of peacefulness

Just know
should darkness appear again with another message
the quicker one pays attention
to the lesson it deems to teach
the faster it will go
never to return

It may be difficult listening the first time
and one does not have to go it alone
by asking for help and guidance if needed
but the process does become easier and easier
for the reward of release is even greater
than the hurt that was felt

Darkness No Longer Rules

It descends upon me once again
and takes me by surprise

After all these years
after all the cleansing
and healing
here I am once again

I have many useful tools now
but which one to use
so I sit and observe the darkness

This is not me
not the light of who I am
the true one within

This feeling is the same
as I first observed it all those years ago
but this time I'm detached enough
to stand back from it
and observe again

I see a covering
and am reminded
that this is but an illusion
not reality of who and what
I truly am

It is a figment of an old pattern
no longer part of my life
a reminder of how far I've come
from my distant past

As I write these words
the darkness is dissipating
because I'm not feeding it with fear
despair or response to pain
even though pain
is contained as part of the memory

Instead I send it love
the best that I can muster
and realize I can do it more easily than ever before

It's going now
Once again it wanted attention
but I didn't respond as I once did

I think it was there to test my faith
to remember all that I've learned
and that I am no longer easily defeated

And for whatever purpose
it came back sitting there
trying to cover up my reality
this time
it did not work

It once showed me how strong I could be
and now it showed me
how strong I've become

And once again
the lesson it taught me
is done

Denial

The more one resists something
the stronger it gets
The more one denies its existence
the longer it lives
The more one runs away from it
the shorter the distance to catch up
The more one takes responsibility for it
the faster one finds release

Depression

The tempest is swirling within me again
just tearing my being asunder
intense and ranging
an internal storm
that is constantly pulling me under

Dreaded feelings exposed to the surface
mixed with turmoil deep-seated inside
it twists and torments and pretends to be
the truths that they cleverly hide

Oh why must I go through these torments
which preys on my strength and my will
it makes life seem darkened and cloudy
I scream to be free from its pull

I yearn for the peace and the freedom
I fight for some calm deep within
but the storm rages on till its passing
if I'm patient I know I can win

The tempest has finally subsided
and with it the knowledge is clear
if I knew not of turmoil and sorrow
I would not know the truths I hold dear

Though just moments ago I was upset
at the damage I thought it had done
I can only now thank you dear tempest
it's through you I have finally won
and the lesson it taught me is done

Note - This was the very first poem I wrote, trying to express to some degree what I was feeling inside. Prior to this I was clueless about why I had these feelings and why they returned intermittently which began in childhood.

I managed to get through these periods, but in early adulthood began to observe they became stronger upon each return until I could no longer ignore it anymore. The ultimate discovery was that within each cycle, emotional pain expressed itself more deeply and intensely to the point of intolerance, until I finally gave it my conscious attention. It became clear that the tempest was inner self screaming to be heard because my heart had, throughout life, learned to swallow how I truly felt inside, eventually losing touch with self and self-expression.

Learning to write down and express what I was feeling started the process and journey of self-discovery that began to put me back in touch with all those feelings long denied. I was in awe that as I wrote what I felt they manifested both in free form and poetry. These expressions became my teacher, showing me the value of paying attention to what I hadn't previously learned through denial.

The journey into emotional pain became worth listening to, not only in rediscovering self, but ultimately in finding that fear and pain are illusions of the mind that one can master and become free from.

Depression – Recognition

Depression for me
has been a belief in limitation or lack
powerlessness
a seed that has grown from early childhood
hidden from view

I had to dig it up
look time and again
to understand why depression
never quite leaves completely

It rears its ugly head from time to time
and lays dormant other times
but I've never fully grasped before
that I am its master
not the other way around

I've seen and labeled it
as disappointed expectation
sadness for not getting my way
of how I pictured it to be

But the bottom line came today
It's about feelings and belief in lack
limitation
a belief in powerlessness or lack of control
hidden deep within lower mind concepts
that fosters a seeming inability to manifest
what I believe will bring me happiness
and diminish what causes unhappiness

With this thought came sadness
for me being disappointed in self

for not grasping how to be happy
or making my life what I desire it to be

as others have seemed to do
Now as an adult
armed with new awareness and knowledge
given an ability to look at everything differently
am ready to make change happen

And so it is

Deprivation and Karma

Today I understood
deprivation

What do I mean?

The realization came
that in many lives I deprived others
of what belonged to them
taken to fill my own cup with more than was deserved
and in this life I have been deprived
feeling at times empty and unfulfilled
coming to understand that depriving others
is not the road towards fulfillment

Greed is a false prophet
one that is never truly fulfilling
It cannot fill the void or emptiness one may feel
only temporarily

Taking from others can only deplete one's soul further
making the void wider
as one becomes more needy
hungry for more

So what am I being shown that will fill the void?

Coming to understand
fulfillment does not come through others
It comes from the Source of all things from within
a gift given to all in life called heart
ours for the asking in rightness
which many do not quite grasp yet

In life we all have been given choice or free will
the power and means to be universally provided for
in what is wanted and needed from an unending source of supply
ours for the asking not for the taking

Was that message not given us
thousands of years ago
by a wise teacher

While meant to be ours for the asking
we have been taught many things
beliefs that block the receiving of it
lack of patience in waiting for it to manifest
or not believing deep within we deserve to have it

There are many who know this
withholding that knowledge from others
to maintain power over them

Thankfully this knowledge is re emerging
becoming more available now
believing deeply from the heart in what is sought
It is knowledge to seek if you haven't already

So what is the lesson?

Those who deprive others for their own gain
will come to know what it feels like
to be deprived
Learn how to fill your own cup to overflowing
so that there is much more to give and share
A way to never feeling deprived again

A truly successful life can only be achieved
through one's own efforts
and if one is still feeling deprived
learn how to look within to find out why

Dichotomy

Dichotomy appears to be
the spice of life
when one is able to view
opposing schools of thought
at the same time

My life often has been filled with dichotomy

Becoming aware
Of inner opposing forces
two sides of the same coin
with different points of view at the same time
not knowing in that moment
what my true feelings are

Has it caused confusion?
You bet!

One side can be the side I wish to experience
And the other side
NOT
Suddenly observing the expression of both sides
appears within moments

I see karma in action
showing me how it was to experience
both sides so I could clearly see
within moments what each side felt like

Examples:
It may show me
how I both hated and was hated
How I was a victim as well as a perpetrator
or similar experiences

And so the brew begins
as feelings of both sides emerge
and merge

Observing and seeing both points of view at the same time
then blends into one
and the understanding provides a sense of forgiveness
when seeing I have been both sides and what each felt like

The spice that inflamed both sides can now simmer
Both sides needed to forgive or be forgiven
so love can now come forth
That's when healing takes place

In this moment I am at oneness
feeling peace with self
at least for the moment

And so the game of dichotomy
continues on with each karmic clearing
of what I had been feeling
leaving me much wiser
than I was a moment ago

Dichotomy and the Third Way

I'm aware
that one day
I may have one point of view
and another day
I may look at the same differently
My feelings about it have changed
two different points of view
existing within me
colliding for domination
of what I truly feel

No wonder
confusion exists
if I can be so changeable

But I've learned through experience
there exists a third way
when the two sides
collide and challenge each other

I can see how I've had
different schools of thought
existing deep in my psyche
in which both or all now emerge
for review
to see with fresh eyes
from a more mature perspective

They now exist side by side
perhaps gleaned from other's points of view
downloaded from as early as childhood
now having the ability to see both points of view
at the same time

becoming blended into one
or what I would call
a third or balanced way

The third way is my current self
making a decision

Two sides become a blending
a marriage between the two different ways
now becoming one
in forming a third way
my way
based on a perspective of now
able to merge from knowledge
learned along the way

I made a decision
and peace exists within
once again

Disappointed Beliefs

In disappointment
frustrations abound
and focus on it will keep it around

The more one believes
the less one achieves
until a more positive focus is found

Discerning Love

Having come to terms
with the seeming lack of love
throughout the threads
of my life
I see the empty spaces

As a child I did not feel love
either coming or going
only expected anticipations
often disappointed

There were those who were loving
but for whatever reasons
it had been easier for me
to love with limitation
harder even to accept love
for what I thought love was
was based out of need
or survival

With nurturing my children
came the first true stirrings
They helped bring forth
what I yearned to do
all my life - -
love freely, fully and happily
as much as I was capable of giving

Here I am many years later
clearly seeing after all these years
the emptiness
the seeming absence of love

or being loved
truly as my own cause
If I was not capable of letting it
flow from the heart
to fill the empty spaces
then how on earth
or heaven
would it ever freely come to me

If we attract as magnets
that which we are
If we receive that which we give
then it makes perfect sense

Only God and I know the reasons
why my heart had been fearful
detached and distanced
and I'm not telling
I only had to make the connection
to allow love to flow freely
to start to fill the empty spaces

Then maybe I'll fully discover
what it feels like to
loving fearlessly
so I may as that magnet
also allowing myself
to be loved
without fear

Discernment

How many times have I felt held back
being kept from having what I wanted
or having something I really liked taken away
or promised something I never received

No matter what the reason
the child in me felt deprived and denied
powerless in believing I could have what I wanted

As adults, one does not realize how they affect
the belief systems of a child or their children

I understand that now by reviewing
patterns in my life that no longer serve me
and at the same time realizing how much I was affected
how much I must have affected my children
while thinking I was doing the best for them
as my parents probably felt
they were doing the best they could for me

This is life being lived unconsciously
not yet aware of how we affect each other and self
in word, thought and deed
beliefs that don't serve us well

I realize even further
that my experience of feeling deprived
was another lesson taught me

Growing up was to deny self of what I wanted
feeling powerless or not worthy enough to have it
grabbing for what I could give to self
that perhaps was not the best for me

such as addictions of food, smoking, etc
others taking it much further in trying to fulfill want
not yet understanding why
Sort of a rebellion of the mind

Thankfully I've come to understand many patterns in my life
enough to change them through discernment
and fulfill self in more positive loving ways
being able to share from that instead of old patterns
yet realizing how strongly old patterns
helped me to understand discernment

Duality

At times I am duality
ambivalent in nature
drawn and repelled
at the same time
trying to find the balance
between the two
to be at peace

For one extreme
is no better than the other
just different sides
to the same story

It takes two sides
to find wholeness
with willingness to combine
the best of both sides
to create balance
and find peace

Echoes

The voices all call out to me
the echoes of my mind
the fragment parts of yesterday
I have not left behind

Like sirens of the Viking days
they sing their songs to me
and beckon with their vision
much a fated memory

And as I wander through my life
the one I am today
the echoes of my lives gone by
still have too much to say

I live my life from day to day
the one that I am now
I want to live it my own way
but echoes tell me how

They conger up the fears and pain
I've suffered long ago
reminding me of yesterday
of everything they know

And if I stop to listen
to the mind of yesterday
I'm only living from the past
and not in my today

Yet echoes have their purpose
and they put me to the test

If I am mindful of their song
they will be laid to rest
The lessons that they deem to teach
call to me in their song
the patterns of my yesterday
will show me what is wrong

If I am not too happy with
the way things are today
I need to heed the echoes
to find what stands in my way

This doesn't mean I need to follow
what is in my mind
but go beyond the thoughts it brings
to seek what I will find

And if I am not mindful
to the gifts they have to give
I'll only join the echoes
in the lives I've yet to live

Effort

Why does it take effort
to go after what is wanted

effort
to eliminate what isn't wanted

and fear of no effort
by having everything
work too easily

Ego Mind Realization

Low self esteem and lack of confidence
is ego mind in judgment of itself
compared to others
too worried about the destination
to enjoy the journey

It reflects all parts of the personality
a whole spectrum of ideas and beliefs
about who and what we seem to be about

Since it isn't easy to see it in ourselves
we see it in others
through the things we like
and especially through what is not liked

a mirrored reflection
a perfect way to see ourselves

Ego Recognition

What is this power within
that can leave a sense of self
feeling helpless and defeated
disappointed or over confident
with the ability to control others
or be controlled by them

We finally come face to face
you and I
who have been at odds with each other
throughout my life

You've gotten me in trouble
time and again
making less than supportive or smart choices
to my well beingness and happiness
to feed ego desires

You, who I've allowed to sabotage my dreams
undo any progressive steps
I could possibly have achieved
blocking my conscious awareness
from seeing you in action
not yet understanding
how you operate

You, a part of my own mechanism
I've finally discovered you
slithering in and out of my life
feeding me distorted truths
and delusions of self
much like the snake

in the story of the Garden of Eden
I see you now
as you are
and no longer choose to listen
unconsciously to the temptations
you often placed before me

I recognize you now
for who and what you are within me
and now that I see you
I'm no longer afraid and am taking my power back!

Yet I thank you for taking on the role of leader
until I came to know you for what you are
for I learned much in the process
and am now ready to be responsible
and take over the helm
realizing as a human I can make mistakes
but can also learn from them
and change direction at any time

Emotional Pain

It's a funny thing about emotional pain
It's true that it's an indicator
a signpost
a guide
something needing to be looked at within
and to deny its existence is to be afraid of fear

The more one runs from it
the longer it hangs around
The faster the acknowledgment
the quicker the freedom from it can come

The saying "it only hurts for a moment"
can be applied to looking at emotional pain
in acknowledging its existence

Once it is looked at it goes and leaves behind a truth
a pearl of wisdom that adds to the richness of ones soul

It's a learning of the highest degree
for the knowledge gleaned from emotional pain
cannot be taught in books

Fear is what darkens its existence and fear is an illusion

Once this truth is realized
the door to discovering truth is opened
and one is guided by the truth of pain
taking steps towards freedom

In using emotional pain as a tool
one finds the strength to forge ahead
even in the darkest moments
towards the light

At times it takes hard work
perseverance
and courage to dig deeper
sometimes just by hanging on by a thread

It is then we are guided the most
with love and understanding
by that which is unseen
also existing deep within us
and is then
when one comes to realize
how strong one can truly be
in the face of seeming adversity

All it takes is the first step
to open the door
with new found courage to continue the journey
when one first comes to see reality
beyond the illusion

Then a seeming enemy becomes a friend
an ally to a better and wiser person
than before
free from the pain of the self
once formerly afraid of

Enlightenment

A funny thing happened
on the way to enlightenment

How became who
Who am I became I am
What am I became I am everything
Where am I became I am everywhere
Why became a crooked letter

Hole became whole
Medication became meditation
Infant became infinite
Constrictive became constructive
Evil became live
Jealousy became lovingly
Fight became fit
Compete became complete
Prey became pray
Atonement became at-one-ment
Become became IS

I no longer choose to believe in
fears of the lower mind
snapshots of time as the only truth
boxes that are limiting
old ways as the only way
for mind and being are multi-dimensional
and far beyond any explanation or single way

Epitaph – But Not the End

This is an epitaph to the old ways
not an ending but leading to
each new beginning

The more layers uncovered
the more I've come to know
that everything had been perfect all along
just the way it was

I've had experiences of darkness
of light
experiences of learning
about both sides of the same coin
each showing me bits of truth about self
the good, bad, ugly
and beautiful

Actually all these are judgments
for I've come to also learn
I Am with nothing added
until I add it

They were experiences
that showed me where I created pain
obstacles or blockages through a belief system
of distortion and illusion
placed there from the onset of early childhood
with lack of understanding the process

Observing and accepting the lessons
is what releases me
from ever having to learn them again

Sometimes it takes courage to listen
and more courage to keep experiencing the pain
until one is willing to see beyond their human experiences
and judgments of them

All they were
were experiences to learn from
providing wisdom through the lessons being taught
but making judgments of these experiences
created the pain
whether through self or others

They taught me much about self
my strengths and weaknesses
which still continues into each day
as I go through metamorphosis or transformation
but thankfully only with a twinge
to get my attention

Some of the major lessons have been
to be less judgmental of self and others
to look inside instead of out to find truth
to seek cause and not focus on effect
and to learn from the wisdom it all provides

I've discovered looking within
one can find more love
peace, happiness, moments of joy
for I've come to really know
that I am whatever I've created
and can change at will
in any given point of time
if I'm not happy with it

. . . but I still have my moments . . .
for I'm only human

Fear

When I say I'm afraid
fearful of a situation
or person who I may feel
can hurt me in some way
what is really being said is
there is lack of recognition
from a point of reference
of not knowing what this is all about
much a stranger to the experience
and not able to take the time to understand
the internal nature behind the fear
in the face of the seeming adversity

What follows is inability
to be in control of the situation
feeling helpless within self
becoming defensive for protection
or looking for a way to appease fear
by giving it more than I willingly wish to
not seeing within
that if I were strong enough in knowing self
what is fearful could never hurt me
or take anything from me

Perhaps I would have something of self
to give to the experience willingly
If I would just take time to understand
what I'm all about
there would be no need
to be fearful
of losing anything

To be afraid of any thing
is to refuse to accept
its existence
as potentially harmless

By running away from it
one judges its nature
without knowing it
perhaps based on old fear
having nothing to do
with now

In the first place
to fear it
is to give that judgment life
To run from it
prolongs its existence
To learn from it
adds to wisdom

To face one's fear within
may take courage
a willingness to accept and understand
perhaps to perceive the reality of it
that it wasn't
something to be afraid of after all
only adding a new dimension
of coming to know
self

Feelings

I sit
not knowing why I feel as I do
Words to describe the feelings
come easily
Reasons for them
elude me
And they sit there waiting to surface
as a bubble waiting to burst
full of hidden emotion
trapped in a lost experience
from time gone by

As the bubble bursts
all the reasons for the experience surface
releasing the emotions
releasing the experience
releasing the lesson it deems to teach
and releasing me
from the pressure of not knowing
who I am

Foreboding and Loving It

I've awakened to
a great sense of foreboding
pure fear
packaged neatly
in the lower mind

It was in my dream
darkness and foreboding
that followed me into
my awakened state

I have not felt so fearful
in such a long time
and I don't know its name
or cause
only where it is within
and what it feels like

I've decided to love it
instead of fearing or listening to it
for I remember now
that darkness cannot live in light
and love is light

It worked -
Bless

Forgiveness

We apparently have two minds
The upper mind Is where our truth flows from
and what we may aspire to be and become

The lower mind is what we have to forgive
be it others or self
The lower mind, if it rambles on
is usually because some type of emotion
or upset is involved

Lower mind will distort truth
in how we perceive others or self
to our liking and righteous satisfaction
often creating misery
in distorted perceptions
especially when choosing to hold on
not willing to let those emotions go
also known as unforgiving

The upper mind is clarity
truth and wisdom
strength
guidance
knowing and freedom
from emotional entanglement and containment
in decision making
in living

Upper mind works with only one ideal
that which we call love

Love just is
and does not hold the heart captive

or block the use of it as not forgiving does
when there is emotional turmoil
in the lower mind

Our free will involves choice
choosing which mind to occupy
on a daily basis
even moment to moment

Make a choice
Live with emotional inconsistency
and instability
or harmoniously through the upper mind
the true one we are meant to be
and truly are

Love is what forgiveness is all about
and the pathway to freedom

Any perceived punishment due
will be acted upon the one considered the perpetrator
through actions of living in cause and effect
by his own hand

A Perception of the Cain Legacy:

I was just shown another perspective to look at in making choice:

Does one choose to live like Cain or Abel
Cain reacted from lower mind and killed Abel
who lived more in the upper mind

It appears that the legacy of Cain
is to live in lower mind until deciding and finding ways
to return to Abel's state of mind
A true allegory?

Forgiveness Again

I asked the Lord
how I could possibly expect to be forgiven
or to forgive self
for the errors I've made
for the seeming sins I've committed
for in my heart I know
in all probability
it may happen again

And in my heart an answer came
How could I know the act of forgiveness
if not to know
the acts to which forgiveness is born

The act of being forgiven
will help me to know
what it's like
so I may be able to forgive
not only self
but others as well

The same holds true
of any other attribute

I felt love come through my heart
as if to taste the wine of a greater truth
I have yet to learn

Freedom

As I become more aware
of the process of unfoldment
As I see myself peal away
layer after layer
to reveal what is truth to me
of who I am and how I operate
returning pieces of me to the whole self
I am in still quite in awe

This whole process
has been quite a journey
painful at times yes
sometimes very painful
often to the edge of precipices
but I have always come back
with true pearls of wisdom
and a freedom not easy to describe

What I ultimately see
heals the wounds
soothes the soul
and puts me in touch with
the idea of a higher intelligence
that has carefully threaded many lifetimes
into an experience of great learning
An understanding of life that runs deep
with perceptions that rise above
pain and suffering

It is true I may have suffered needlessly
but not totally in vain
for it has motivated me in the direction

to get rid of it
to understand why it was there
and to release it
from ever being there again

Not all suffer so deeply
Not all have to
I don't fully know why I chose this path
but am happy to "know" that I am on it
and that there truly is love
support and guidance
to help light the way
away from suffering

I am happy and thankful to have tools
to hone and reshape
restructure the patterns that kept me stuck
to make a beautiful place I want to live in

Each layer has revealed pearls of wisdom
as to who I am
and why I have been
or acted as I did

I've seen how it has all
ultimately been my doing
not others
Others have all reflected me
to show me the way
to more of self

I've truly learned
that the whole trip is to learn
forgiveness
and to love self
beyond all else

For when that is accomplished
one can truly begin
to have those moments
of love and forgive others
and become fully free
happy
fulfilled and whole

One cannot fully describe the wondrous joy
that lies beneath
that silently and patiently awaits our return

I've quite a ways to go to get there
but along the way I am given tastes
as much as I can accept
that my being will allow

This too motivates me
especially when I am aware and
diving into the darkness
to reveal the light
It's what keeps my head above it all
my lifeline
so I don't get lost in it

And why do I continue put myself through this willingly
(though sometimes I still kick and scream along the way)
Because I have seen the outcome
with these moments now further apart and lighter than before
As they lead me towards freedom
with more moments of happiness in life

Freedom in Action

We've just met
and yet
you've touched the beast in me

I wonder why
and then I try
to look within at what I see

It's not out there
but deep in here
that stirs the way I feel

I can't yet see
what it can be
but it seems so very real

What brought this on
I wish you gone
and you're still standing there

And here am I
Responding, why?
it's more than I can bear

But do I see
the you in me
that caused this angry flow

And you can bet
I'll feel upset
until I let this go

It's not out there
but deep in here
that holds the freedom key

And once I know
what caused this flow
then I can set it free

and bring back peace to me

Give and Take

Take the time to do it right the first time
so it doesn't have to be done
over and over again

Give it all the caring and love
and attention you have
to become a master builder
a master creator

Giving

How can I love thee
if I do not first know love within

How can I respect thee
if I do not first respect self

How can I know thee
if I do not first know self

I can only give to thee and others
from the storehouse of that
which I have reaped
from the bounty
of that which I have sown

Giving One's Power Away

If one grew up feeling loved
secure in who they are
they have sensed their own power
from within

However
if one did not thrive
in such an environment
one may continually
seek to find power
by viewing themselves
through the eyes of others
giving their power to another
to provide what they think
may be missing within
themselves

Perhaps all they want to feel
is love, security and respect
to know they are cared for
and important to others

Too bad they don't yet understand
that their true power
comes from within
before giving it away
to get what they already have

Golden Light - 1

I inwardly saw a glimmer of light

I had heard of the golden light
but to my surprise
it was really golden

What is this wondrous thing
that has revealed itself to me
I watched it in awe
much like a child who
has seen something new for the very first time

I felt a giggle inside
more of an inner smile
It felt good to be in it
It didn't stay very long
but that's okay
I know from experience it will return now and then
more and more
until I permit it to always be there

I don't yet know its true nature
but as the dark clouds have taught me to listen
I know this too will reveal itself to me
in the lightness it is
as time goes by

Golden Light - 2

Another light episode
a golden glow within
this time touched with a glimmer of "Divine"
an indescribable light
much like a twinkle of magical stardust

Again it did not stay long
more like a gentle reminder
of its existence

It reminds me of Tinkerbell
grown up
And even in these first tastes
I sense it is only playfully toying with me now
until I am ready to receive more

Grief and Grieving

Grief is an expression
of what is felt when something or someone
is lost

In the beginning grief is strong
possibly filled with many emotions
sorrow
hurt
emptiness
shock
disbelief
anger
a sense of loss or longing

One may experience many things
during periods of grief
for there is no rhyme or reason
when it appears
or length of time
one grieves

Waves of emotion may hit
from the depths of ones being
during the most unexpected moments
and last for minutes
hours
days

All one can do
is take the opportunity
to grieve as deeply as one needs to
feel the emotion

feel the pain
cry the tears
Experience what is being felt
fully and completely
without judgment
for this is a cleansing process
and then let it pass when it's done

Over time the grief will lessen
as well as the intensity of emotions

To ignore grief
is to invite it to return once again
carrying those emotions ignored
only having to experience them again
until they are acknowledged

Be kind and gentle with yourself
during these moments
for you are the one hurting
and the good memories you wish to keep
will still remain with you

Guilt

There have been many shoulds and should nots
taught to me in my life
in addition to the Shalts and Shalt Nots
to guide my way

I've also been taught to accept things
the way they are
whether or not I liked it
and to be thankful for the way it is
and count my blessings
because it could be much worse
in the ways of the world

I guess this is true
but something was lost in the translation
I could never quite fathom until now

No one ever taught me how
to deal with the thoughts and feelings which arose
that I wasn't supposed to be feeling
as a result of following this philosophy
Instead of understanding why they were there
I began to feel guilty
for having thoughts and feelings less than virtuous
and punished self in many ways for it

In addition to the punishment and reward received for my
    actions
and the guilt felt for not living up to expectations
I always felt like I walked a tightrope
not quite grasping the why of it all
only that I should or should not
can or cannot

What seems to have been lost in the translation
is understanding the why of it all
not having been given explanations along with commands

Punishment, reward and guilt kept me from knowing
a choice could be made for self
by talking responsibility for my mistakes
to find the meaning behind it
in order to make my own decisions to learn from

Shalt and Shalt Not are creeds to live by
Shoulds and should nots are sometimes born
out of fear from experiences of others
perhaps warnings to be considered
not to be decided by self
and then there are those as those lovely
can and cannots . . .

If honesty was more rampant than virtuousness
I suppose I might have saved myself much misery
yet out of ignorance
I've been guilty of the very same

Happiness

Just a few simple words. …

True happiness comes from within
and is not governed by what happens
or does not happen out there

It is not measured by the action or
non-action of others

It is happiness from within
that brings forth happiness without
not the other way around

If one really seeks to be happy
it begins with listening
to what your true self is telling you

True self is the best friend you'll ever have
in all the world

Hopelessness to True Happiness

Woke up this morning to a sense of hopelessness
another aspect of darkness hidden within a corner of lower mind
born from experiences, imprints and memories
in lifetimes of suffering
from beliefs formed that bred experiences
of non-achieving, non-receiving
not having being given or having things taken away
caught up in a world of seeming lack and limitation
wealth for some and not for others
creating a conglomeration of limitation and hunger
to be enslaved and caged by
perhaps an experience by many in the world of now
still caught in memories of darker times or what is not yet known
still active in creating feelings of "what's-the-use" moments
giving up the fight by no longer believing in other possibilities
and hurting for it

Having long observed the cause of suffering within
a world of hurtful memories and feelings of separation
this feeling rose once again to affect my world of now
yet now able to safely explore this sense of hopelessness

Something then shifted
In the world of today there is new movement
using love and light from within to transform darker feelings
with new teachings of hope and a vision of a greater world
all created from within by changing perspectives

Exploring further
it was like observing a phoenix rising from the ashes
for what was observed in feeling hopeless
was but a covering to the true source of inner wealth

Observing many lives in a world of those who sought riches
and power through ego-based self worth by owning things
like precious metals of gold, silver
money sometimes used for good and other times for power and
    greed
using ego-based beliefs to create illusions of being better than
over those who didn't have a sense of self worth
always seeming to want more yet never feeling fully satisfied

You know the ones who are easily misled
Those who believe out there is the only place to find a way to exist
often seeking approval or working for others who appear to own
    wealth
surviving through rules set by them
while manifesting self-judgmental experiences
based on inner beliefs
of lack

I was then shown where true wealth exists
a golden light of being beneath it all inside of me
This awakening revealed it always existed
but no longer seen or felt beneath the coverings
that created feeling broken
supported through many lifetimes
of recreating and responding to lack and not empowerment
instead of building dreams to create through Source

I observed true inner wealth is meant to be shared with others
from the bounty of my being
instead of trying to grasp it from out there

And so the true source of gold is within
the power where happiness and fulfillment exists
that nothing out there can buy or be taken away
unless allowing self to become separated once again from its
    existence
I finally get it!

Humble Humble

I'm a new breed of humble
as soon as I see a truth
that has tempered the ego
and humbly accept what I truly am
I become much like the athlete
and get off the bench to go in for more

Many times I've read or heard
of people who had light experiences in one felt swoop
Their whole life changed
and they seemed to live happily ever after
mastering their lives
with new found faith and awareness

Mine has been gradual
a buildup of many years of hard work
and perseverance
and I'm still going strong

I must admit
each humble has made it easier
to face the next part of me

I do see changes in my life
internally and externally
long-term
not overnight

Each realization
has changed my life
day to day
moment to moment
and each has been special

I've come to value the process of soul
and to give up parts of my ego for it

Maybe there is a "big one"
or maybe just a bunch of little ones
It probably doesn't matter how long it takes to get there
as long as we get there
wherever and whatever that is

Hunger

There are different
kinds of hunger
besides food

Hunger for love
hunger for acceptance
hunger for freedom
hunger for friendship
  or relationships
hunger for fulfillment
and many more

These can be the true causes of hunger within
that we try to feed every day

Sit down and see what hungers
may be related to you

Acknowledge each of them
and let understanding come

Nourish yourself with kindness and love
Fill the void of need
and watch the pain of hunger
become peaceful
and fulfilled

I Am Whole, I Am Sovereign, I Am Free

What do these words mean to me . . . a lot!

It means I am not a compartmentalized human
one trapped in a world of different feelings and dualities
thoughts and ideas that determine what actions to take
questioning who I am on a daily basis
based on how I feel when I awaken and open my eyes

Every day is different
yet sometimes feeling it's the same as yesterday
actually many yesterdays
but after a long journey, a very long journey
have come to realize I have felt alone and not supported
trying to remember and be all that I knew I once was
but seemingly forget momentarily

I've asked self time and again
from moments of experiences that showed me inner truth
moments of just being without judgment or thought
in a state of mind that is peaceful
Why can I not seem to stay in those moments permanently
especially after having realized many new beginnings
only ending up having to begin again
even after all the experiences I've been through in life
still allowing emotions to play a big role in how I feel
that once formed perspectives and judgments to live life by

Each day I awaken and move through the experiences of that day
knowing I have the power to change what no longer seems to
    work
whatever my mind and body are feeling if less than happy
but often forget and just live in the emotions instead of observing
    them
that can determine outcomes based on effects of cause

Frankly I'm tired of struggle
not with others but within self
sitting here in the moment of now asking questions
Why if I know how to just BE and let go
do I keep getting involved in feelings that affect actions I take
and not just BE in every moment of knowing
    having done it many times before
yet find easy to fall out of and forget momentarily
    that I have the power to change it

Perhaps this is what is meant when said Falling Out of Grace
yet just as easy to put self back into it
when becoming aware again and remind myself that I can

At times I have felt very alone on this journey
not because I miss being surrounded by others
but because I miss being supported by my own being
experiencing wholeness, sovereignty and freedom
instead of continually attempting to heal self
when reminded of past emotional wounds carried
instead of letting go to move past these emotional springboards
the ones that seem to control life

The blessing is coming to recognize the patterns
aware more and more of what is being felt
keeping in mind that the state of being in grace
leads to wholeness sovereignty and freedom
always having the power and ability to put myself there
when becoming aware I'm not in it and still needing reminders

Perhaps it's part of mastery in the art of becoming
somehow needing reminders that practice helps to endure
much like a musician who must practice to master his instrument
In order to learn how to play the perfect masterpiece called
I Am Whole

I Am Sovereign
I Am Free
. . . just BE

Ignorance (Ignore-ance)

I see how much my own ignorance
has caused me to suffer
beyond necessity
not particularly out of stupidity
but of choice to ignore other possibilities
choosing to label everything in a neat package
attempting to know what to expect in advance
so I could react with much control
sometimes refusing to see many other sides
of the same experience by making things fit
into my picture of what was wanted

I set limitations beyond necessity
and if things did not work according to preconceived notions
the unknown became fearful

I see how there can be more sides to one idea
more than two sides
a wide spectrum between opposite ideas
(which perhaps are but one idea)
the reality of the way things are in any given moment
not always the same reality from everyone's perspective

To accept that there is more
to any given situation than the eyes or senses can see
or that previous experience has shown
is to begin to trust a greater reality
and source of knowledge to safely guide my way
through many possibilities

Perhaps this is the cause of ignorance
the choice not to listen to the inner guide
or to ignore
and blindly follow ego

Image

Out of the world of ideas
feelings, beliefs
comes thoughts
decisions
of what it is I wish to be
spawned out of
what it is I don't wish to be
seeing two sides
choosing one over the other
having taken my five senses
and used them
to build an image

It's what I wish all of you
to see me as
and what I want
to believe is me
to live successfully in this world
to be a part of it

My mind has done a good job
building the image
out of want, need
and a desire to be
all the good qualities
I've observed available

I've used acknowledgment
to feed the image
pulling from outside sources
changing what doesn't
seem to work
for what does

I've used every outside acceptable idea
to be for you what I think you want
to gain for me what I think I want

I've kept a wall of seeming confidence and stability
to keep you from seeing
my fears and doubts
my face, eyes and actions
not showing my true feelings

Instead of being me
what I have gained is an image
some of which is part of
who I truly am
But it's up to me
to prove to myself from within
that I'm worthy to keep it
if it's what I really want
it to be

Importance

I'm beginning to realize that some things cannot hurt me
if not placing a high value of importance on them
This is what seems to produce and feed negative feelings
such as fear of loss, failure, jealousy
all that could feed an ego mind
if it doesn't quite work out as planned

The word importance is very powerful
When placed on an object, thing or person
it immediately stands out from the background
indicating something of value is more important
than everything else
which may lead to want of possession
or leading to fear of loss

When this is done
lesser value is placed on the background
from which importance stemmed from
This could indicate self and others as well

Instead of looking to make one part important
by separating it from the whole
is it possible that looking at the whole as important
will include all in the value

Perhaps oneness means looking at everything
from this point of view

It's called Love

In Here – Not Out There !

If anyone comes to read this
that does not yet know
the truth of the mirror
then I don't know
the words that will help you
to perceive this truth

I can only say
take heart in your struggles
with others
with self
Freedom is at hand
It's only a matter of acceptance and understanding
and truth lights the way

Be not afraid
to look at self
Be not afraid
to admit what is fearful
Be not afraid
of telling self what is true
even if ego dreads to admit it

For that is where true freedom lies

That is where external struggle begins and ends -
within

That is where to look

Insights Along the Way

- ☀ There is time a to participate and there is time to step back and observe, but being passive is not facing one's reality or responsibility

- ☀ I am the solution to my problem

- ☀ Will the real being within please stand up and shine

- ☀ Believe to achieve and receive

- ☀ Let attitude be gratitude

- ☀ Emotional victimhood is a state of mind that keeps one from taking the responsibility of caring for self

- ☀ What you welcome will come – that goes for every single thing

- ☀ Peace is a quiet acceptance of who one is as one is in any given moment with nothing added

- ☀ Thoughts and emotional responses are what brings one to experience a positive or negative result

- ☀ Running away from pain is to keep self imprisoned. It will just be carried wherever you go

- ☀ Seek the truth within the darkness and you will find the light

- ☀ It has been said that home is where the heart is – and I carry mine wherever I go

Integration

Sometimes
shadows of yesterday
fragments of unhappy memories
and long forgotten emotions
come to haunt my awareness

I now gently remind them
and myself
who I am now
and what is my truth

I hug them within myself
tell them its all right
show them what I know they can be
and then watch their concerns slowly disintegrate
and integrate
into the one I am
now

Intention

Intention is
moment to moment
a choice that is made
with each step taken in a direction
whether it be
for self
for the good of all
for greed or avarice
good or evil
or any other purpose

Intention is
singularity of mind
in taking any action
with intent of purpose

The purpose dear reader
is up to you
from moment to moment

May you choose wisely

Jigsaw Puzzle

Every time I get that feeling
the one that alerts me
that it's time to go inside
and see what may be sad
what may be angry
what may be ambivalent
or a part of me that feels separated
I now take the call right away

I can no longer identify my being
as separated
for each time I've faced a fear
hurt or darkness
a truth is discovered inside
and the release from it
provides a feeling of freedom
a deep sigh of relief

A sense of unburdening if you will
takes place
the piece once hidden in darkness
is now restored
providing an another piece
to the puzzle of me

Journal of Smiles

I realize how much more I smile from within these days
genuinely

I can't yet say my world is perfect
but far better than it used to be

I'm still challenged
constantly
and have come to see and accept
that life is a challenge in itself
only
being fully armed with the right tools
makes it easier to move through it
and stronger to be who I am

I'll look back a year from now
and see where I've been
Right now all I can see is where I am
leading to where I'm going

I bet that I'll have far more to say
on the subject
since that's what growing up is all about
But I will say that it's more fun
having a smile as my companion on this journey
than the dark clouds of yesterday

When the "dc's" come now
I listen quickly so they'll go away faster
and they do

That alone makes me smile
and a lot wiser than I was only moments before

Judgment

Everyone has their own truth
To accept another's point of view
even though it may differ from our own – on any level
does not have to make our point of view wrong
in the face of his or hers

Each person sees truth in their own way
perhaps from viewing the subject
from different perspectives or points of viewing
based on the angle they see it from
and one who feels strong enough in his convictions
does not need to force their position upon another

Judgment is rejecting what has not been seen
by the person judging who may need proof to accept it

To look down upon another's truth
is to judge it
To listen to and understand
or accept another's view
is to possibly see another part of the whole
another side to the story

Doing this does not make either side right or wrong
but to be able to accept
a larger truth
is to see
the Creator in all

Karma

In karma
anything I do now
sets the future in motion
It's the way I do it
that seems to determine what the experience will be
So perhaps
I need to pay more attention
to how I respond to present experiences
of my own making

Knowing

What is it
Where does it come from
Does it have dimension
Is it something we can touch

It is a voice of wordless words
A spark within
that reaches out to us
from the depths of our being

When observing outside sources
it says within
I know this to be or not to be true for me
without having to judge
whether or not it is

It exists at the true source
of our beingness
a gift
from the depths within us
once we quiet our minds enough
to hear it

Some may call it intuition
but the voice is more than a feeling
for it has a form of expression
something that's hard to describe
or fathom
unless one experiences it

Mind glosses over it
with incessant chatter
questions

ego driven decision-making
judgments
all covering the true essence
of who we are
and what is

Bottom line . . .
If you learn to let go
you will come to "KNOW"

Knowledge of Spirit

I was taught
to first accept possibilities
then knowledge will come

From knowledge comes understanding
From understanding comes truth
From truth comes knowing
and from knowing comes wisdom

That's a seeming process
to begin the journey
towards opening the door
to what some call becoming spiritual

Acceptance is not a matter of belief
To accept is acknowledging an existence
based on possibility or concept
and a way to bypass what the naked eye can't see
without requiring a form
or proof to be submitted

One is just saying
the existence is possible
without requiring one to declare
belief or non belief in it

Once allowing possibilities
broader views will begin to appear
more doors will open leading to
more knowledge on the subject(s)
allowing one to make informed decisions
on whether or not to believe it and then live by it

A sense of truth existing within us
allows one to come to know from within
through wordless words
from an inner perception
truth speaking to our conscious mind
as our soul goes through
a process of unfoldment
for we already have the knowledge
existing deep within us

One just has to remember
by allowing self to start receiving it
without requiring external proof

It is much like a rose
Each petal unfolds
perfectly
revealing the light
of its inner beauty as it does

One cannot seek their core
until the petals of our soul
begin to unfold to reveal it
and while something one may not be able to prove
one can behold the beauty that exists beneath it all
from within
and shine it brightly to the outer world

Lament

The more one laments the experience they're in
resists it
in action
in mind
the more it will continue
to manifest

One can change the action
first through acceptance
giving to it the best they can
to learn from the experience
then let it go

That way
one can start allowing themselves
to receive more loving experiences

It's the Law of Attraction

Layers

One important thing
I've learned over the years
from each realization
epiphany
or moment of truth
is that each discovery may be part of many layers
covering up other parts
more deeply ensconced in its expression
and the knowledge it brings

Uncovering the layers are part of the process
of taking steps towards deeper understanding
awakening to perceptions
of other facets of the same experience
from different perspectives
to eventually reach the whole of it

In letting each layer go
much like peeling petals of a closed flower
(or in my opinion sometimes like an onion)
leads to the finer layers
of beingness and wholeness

Once fully realized
the lesson is done
. . . and on to the next one

I may even see what I learned
differently years from now
as each layer is but a step
towards a greater truth
and freedom

Life

I studied long and hard and thought I knew it all
So I said, "Here I am, I'm ready, where is the light?"
and nothing came
I waited for hours, days, months, years
and still nothing
Realizations came and went
like the tide rushing in and out
When the tide came in I said, "This must be it!" but then
it went out and left me as before
The next time it came in, my knowing grew deeper than before
new dimensions appeared
but still no light
As it ebbed away, I was lower in spirit than before
I built a beacon for the light and began searching again
I re-studied, believed anew
I saw a large wave in the distance and sure enough
it hit me even stronger than before . . .
passing away just as quickly
I waited again
nothing came
I decided to pack it in and forget the whole thing
Time passed and just as I thought it was all okay
I fell deeper into darkness
The wave came suddenly and hit me with all its power
Deeper understanding and knowing
and still no light
This time it didn't seem to matter
As the wave slipped away I wondered what it was that I
    seemed to know
I could not remember, yet
it was still there with me
I suddenly thought, "What am I looking for anyway?
How can I find what I already have"
I cried out with all my being "I AM THE LIGHT"
And the tide rushed in and out as before whispering "Just Be"

Light Beingness

I Am a being of light
that shines more brightly every day
through effort on my part
to let it shine

It always has been a process of development
and still is
For the more I invite the light into my life
the brighter will it become within me
to shine forth out into the world

And if even for a moment I forget
and focus on an emerging shadow within
(which thankfully diminishes more and more)
I have only to quickly remind myself
to process quickly and think of the light
or the many reminders that surround me

I can see more clearly
each time I stop to take a look
at the progression that unfolds
both within and without

It is a beautiful process to behold
for as I allow more light to fill my being
I feel more whole
happy and complete

I become more aware every day
that this journey of discovery is far from over
and that I must continually make the effort to achieve
    accomplishment
to achieve well beingness

and often wonder why light is the hard part to maintain
with shadow the easier one to fall back into
Perhaps it is a never-ending process
but I know I must go forward and make every effort I am
    capable of
without judgment
for I certainly don't ever wish to return
to where this journey first began

Limitation

I've kept myself boxed in a corner
settling for less than what I want
wanting more
than what I believe I could have
living in the mind
a dream world of "if only's"

It's been safe there
willing to accept the pain of disappointment
rather than leave the corner
to experience the dream

I've begun to realize what kept me there
was wanting for the wrong reasons

I believed I couldn't have what I wanted
so I settled for less
because that's what I really believed of me
compared to the way I wished it to be
The wishing itself made me believe it wasn't so

Rather than wanting to live the experience
and learn from it
and what it had to teach in self-discovery
I thought I lacked the ability
not confident enough to take risks

The mind built pictures
of how I wished to be
to prove me wrong
but in reality it hardly ever came true
because I really didn't believe it possible

What I've settled for
is a world of dreams
in my mind
to live in a reality of disappointment
going after what I think it is I want
and willing to take lesser things
as consolation
sometimes even having given up
some of my self-respect
to make even a small part of the dream
a seeming reality

What I've really done
is to settle for a corner
instead of willingness to be
part of the experience
of it all

Live in Now

When one is in the process of thinking
he is not experiencing self
he is in the mind
living in past or future

Bring self into the experience of now
and share life together

Acknowledge self for what it is
not run away from it
by hiding in the past or future of the mind
for that is how one punishes self
and suffers for it

Acknowledge self for what it is
bring it into your experience of now
and you are united

Loneliness

I live among people
like one lone star
in a vast sky of multi-billions
at times feeling lonely and lost
yearning to be heard
understood
counting on countless others to fill the void -
an emptiness inside
expecting them and my outer surroundings
to remove the pain of living
I much created for self

At times anger and bitterness
move in to fill the void
tempered with fleeting moments of joy and happiness
changing from day to day
sometimes moment to moment

I would feel good or dislike myself
shifting these emotions on the tide of outside influence

Suddenly realizing what is needed
to fill the emptiness
is to love, respect and accept unconditionally
my inner being first
above all others
for others cannot do that job for me

I cannot expect more from myself
than what is there to offer
especially if my cup is far from filled
or expect more from others

than they have to offer me

Once accomplished
no one can hurt me
for I have been my own worst enemy
in hurting self
no one else

To accept my being
is to become complete
able to give freely of what there is
to others
accepting freely
what they want to offer me
without demand or expectation

There is no longer a need
to be anything but who I am
and if I feel loneliness
then I am its cause

Love – What Is It ?

Love Is Love

Love shows no favoritism
no judgment
no retaliation
no hunger
no pain
no worth or value

Love just is

When one can learn to love all as is
finding ways to open festering wounds
cleansing the contents of past hurts and feelings
judgments
all that was repelled in thought in mind and feeling
that stood in the way
one will come to know the source of true love

It is within each and every one of us
and we each hold the key
to opening the floodgates of our hearts

If we can learn to love all as is (even self)
through the loving Law of Allowance
forgiveness will abound
joy will be found
and love will abide

It is the true way to contribute to healing
not only self
but the world as well

Love and Self Esteem

The very hardest lesson I've ever had to learn
perhaps from lifetimes
is that no experience
no person or thing
should ever ever ever ever ever

                                          ever

affect how I feel about self

Too often I've let "out there" affect "in here"

Too often I've judged self
based on what came to me
… or didn't
where I stood in the seeming chain of command
… looking up towards or down at
how I was treated and by whom
… and how much
all instruments of measurement
of self love
of self worth

And today
after all the years of knowing the concepts
after working so hard to heal my ego, mind and emotions
I finally got it
It reached my heart …
"worldly things can't measure love
my heart gives it for free"

Nothing can take this love away from me
from giving it to self
unless I give it permission

156

Now to me, this should be a cause for celebration
since I've reached another pinnacle
And yet
my heart tells me that nothing is different
This is the way it should always be
and the way it always was

I just had to remember it

Love Source

Today I'm standing
on the side of my emotions
clearly aware
that if I had not felt loved
I had not felt loving

If I had not been successful
I had not felt successful

When there were angry situations
it was I who felt the anger or responded to it

My emotions have painted pictures for me
to experience my feelings
or not

It was entirely my choice

If I want to be loved
then I must find love within me to give it
If I want to be successful
then I must first feel that I am successful
And if I don't want angry situations in my life
then I must find forgiveness of the anger within

It's all up to me
isn't it

Messages

Everyone receives messages
from on high
all the time
but ego the lower mind
seeks to block them
and remain master through darkness
hurt and pain

One just has to learn to listen
with a different set of ears
the truth from within the core of ones being

Did you ever hear a song
playing over and over in your head

Take time to listen to the words
That song is a message for you
no one else

Listen –
do the words ring true for you
in that given moment
or are you just being told
you are loved

And listen to that which comes through your heart
your soul is speaking to you

Mirror Images

Simply said
the mirror
is a measure
of what work must be done

If to me "out there" is moody
or cloudy and dark
I have some inner work to do

If to me the sun is shining
and all things bright and happy
then I get to go out
and enjoy it

Music From My Soul

When I dance
I soar in spirit
in mind
in loving light

The music from without
touches the music within
my body moves and sways
my feet takes my body to other places
my arms express feeling

I am whole
I am happy
and if I am not
music will make it so if I let it

I can move my body
and be who I wish to be

I can close my eyes and be myself
fully and completely
and all is good

I can be sad
I can be happy
and it matters not
who and what I am
or what I look like

When I dance from within
I am different from no other
I am who I am

and nothing else matters

Negativity

Negativity is an illusion
of the mind
not a life force
in its own right
It is only kept alive
when nurtured with attention
an invitation to be there
again and again
Let it go and it will fade away
into
oblivion

Focusing on the positive
is inviting those qualities
into your life
It is already there
for it is life itself
Welcome it with open arms
acknowledge it
give freely of its nature
and it will grow stronger
into Beingness

Non-Beingness

I once described the wonderful state of being
of allowing everything to BE
what it is
as it is

It was a lovely experience that I had
a gift to see how wonderful life is
as I allow my self to BE

And then I seemingly lost it
when I tried to convince another to BE
for I gave it away instead of just being
instead of just enjoying my gift

Today I realized what non-beingness is
It is living in a state of wanting
of not wanting
of thinking what is and isn't
what was and wasn't
what will be or not

Desire is always rampant
accompanied by an emotional roller coaster
of ups and downs
all based on getting what is wanted
or not getting it
and based on getting what isn't wanted
Even getting rid of what isn't wanted

Self-esteem is tied into it also
for if one gets what they want how great it is
and if not where did that self esteem go

And how often does one get everything they want
Non-beingness is non-trusting
It is mind saying "I decide what's right and not right"
Instead of asking "is this right for me"
and having to deal with the consequences when they come
It is also not allowing what is to be what is

I've been in both states and have been taught
that one needs to experience the shadow side to know the
    light
and yet
I wonder how much of it is conscious choice
or part of a master plan

Does it really take an opposite side to know
how wonderful it could be on the other side
To feel that something is lost - - even for a moment
when not having it after beautifully experiencing it
to learn to appreciate having been there
after not knowing it existed in the first place?

Is it a lesson to be learned or a consequence of action?
Or is it another what is…is?

Opportunities

Today I recognize an opportunity
similar to one that came before
when I was a young girl
It said to me then
"here is your opportunity
to be different
to change what you don't like in yourself
and become what you do like
and want to be"
and I took the opportunity back then

We moved away
and I left behind much I didn't like
and offered myself a new way
a clean slate to start anew
as much as I was capable of
at that time

I'm not saying every day
is not an opportunity
it is
very much
It just seems once in awhile
life offers us the real big ones
and today is one of them
and I'm taking it

Thank you God

Pain – A Storyteller

Pain can be a storyteller
a motivator
Is it not?

Does it not get one's attention (eventually)
that there may be something to look at
to find out cause
to see where it's indicator is directing to

Some think it's due to illness
Injury
emotional upset
and rightly so
but there are many levels and dimensions to pain

If one is willing to look deeper
one will find pain is both motivator and storyteller

It grabs your attention to look deeper
Inviting you to find out why it's there
or how it came to be

However some run away and cover it up
thinking it's the enemy
and not truly understanding its purpose

Running will only make it worse
for it will always return
possibly even stronger
until one is tired of running
and is ready to pay attention

Pain can be an indicator that something is wrong
within body/mind and spirit

But how many actually understand
that pain is generated as a manifestation
of pain in the soul
something that needs to be tended to

If one stops running and learns to listen
pay attention and ask questions
soul will communicate what is needed
and true healing will begin

Parents

Our parents are great teachers
chosen with care and wisdom
before we came back to life
to work out our issues
and learn truth
about ourselves
through mirroring images

Our parents have their own issues
who we chose to closely align with ours

We learn through observation
strongly believing at times
that they are cause of our pain
when in truth
we were already in pain
and they only reminded us

They are reflectors
mirrors to learn from since we can't
always see who we are
by ourselves

Thank and bless them
for what they teach offers opportunities
of seeing self and what is within

Perhaps there is deep respect for them
wanting to reflect those qualities
in your life

Or perhaps response to them
Is with less than loving feelings

of what is not wanted
What are their lessons teaching you?

Look within to find what part of self
is complaining
What is it that offends you and why

They offer opportunities
to learn what you both wish and don't wish
to have in your life

Perhaps there is a lesson to be learned
or an old pattern that needs attention
that reminds you of their actions

Once done the floodgates
of forgiveness and love will open
both for them and for you
providing the opportunity
to fill the emptying spaces
with what is wanted
that once housed another illusion

And believe it or not
once changing your own pattern of response
your parents will change as well

I've seen it happen
many times

Peaceful Mind

The mirror of my mind is clear today
I see it wafting
gently
like a pool of still water

If I were to drop a pebble
it would ripple in response

If I were to drop a rock
it would become turbulent

But now it's peaceful
and I'm enjoying it

Perceptions of the Mind

I realize now
what this book has truly been about

Not about how wonderful
moments of the light are
(though it is)
and not so much about struggle and pain
but more about overcoming it
fully meeting the challenges that life presents
and
what taking responsibility
for self and my actions means

To discover that I have the strength to be cause
and can take responsibility for the direction of my life
To stop lamenting mistakes and put self back on track
by learning from them

This is a wonderful feeling
because at times it has been hard work and took great effort
but it has been worth it
and I feel very blessed
to know this
and be where and who I am

This alone has made the continuing journey much easier

Potential

Last night
I saw a man and thought
what a wonderful mind he had
but felt he had so much potential
he didn't use
I observed a mind
with great possibilities
troubled
and therefore
not using it to its fullest potential

Today
I turned around on the spectrum
and looked the other way
and saw a mind
that had great potential
There was so much out there
to know
and it was not being used
to its fullest potential

That mind is mine

Poverty of Mind

As I have looked upon the world
through awakening eyes and heart
I've begun to see
how the world reflects the mind
much as a teacher

I've come to observe both inner and outer worlds
for as I experience one
it reflects the condition of the other

Stepping out of darkness into light
has given me many new perspectives
to change my way of thinking
of being
of becoming
all through observation

Today the lesson was poverty - -
observing both poverty in the world
and my reactions to it

I observed that poverty is more than an outward condition
It is a state of mind - -
Poverty in the world is a reflection
of a mind in poverty

There is poverty of loving and respecting self
of ones thinking poorly of themselves
Some are afraid to give freely from ones own storehouse
because it is believed that the supplies are limited
and there may not be enough left
if it were given away

I also saw that one can turn poverty of the mind
to prosperity of the mind
so the reflective mind may bring forth prosperity to the world
to the collective mind
therefore diminishing poverty in the world more and more

Have you not already seen the world changing
For as one learns to give more freely from themselves
without fear
more is regenerated
and there is more that can be given away
whether it be love, respect, money

It is all connected anyway to the reflective mind
So may all find true abundance within their own hearts

By the way this is not a new concept
just one that more and more are awakening to
each and every day

Prayer for Direction

I do not wish to live in darkness any longer

I do not wish to be held back anymore
from experiencing my full potential

I do not wish to sit at the foot of the mountain
of non action due to fear
afraid to move forward
of what I might find
of making mistakes

I do want to feel gratitude
freedom
and appreciation for my life more and more
accepting all that I truly am

I do want to be fearless of making mistakes
knowing that all mistakes are teachers
that can lead to greater truths

I do want to experience my full potential
through love, light and happiness

Keep showing me the way ....

With loving appreciation

Thank you

Prayer of Thanksgiving

Each morning I light candles
in prayer and blessings
to all that directs my life
guides me and provides for me

I give thanks the Creator, to God
to the Divine of all there is
to all who touch my life
in so many ways
to all who teach me
and pray
for all who may be in need
to find their way

Learning to say "thank you" is
truly a blessing
Sometimes it's an expression
of deep gratitude
and other times
it is a reminder of what I have
when I need to be reminded

The light flickering on the candle
is a gentle reminder
of all that is good and true in my life
and how truly blessed
I am

Rebirth

The caterpillar spins its cocoon
isolating itself from the world
for a period of time
to emerge a beautiful butterfly
wings spread to fly
to experience new things

What happens to its being
from the moment it enters the cocoon
and metamorphous begins
to change its physical structure
to something completely different
than what it used to be

Does its being change
to accommodate the new freedom coming
Must it learn how to fly
from its very depths to give it courage
to explore and experience anew
after being slow and deliberate
and earthbound
or does it simply let go of the old
to make way for the new

When it finally does emerge
is it the caterpillar transformed
or a butterfly - reborn

Receiving

Throughout my life
there seems to have been
much connected to the subject of receiving
pain carried somewhere within
many tapes stored and connected to many facets
of the same truth

There is pain of receiving
and not feeling worthy enough

Pain of receiving
and not feeling capable of returning in kind

Pain of disappointment
in not receiving what is wanted or asked for
or not in the time frame it was asked for

Pain in receiving
and not liking what is being given

Pain of receiving
feeling that something will be expected in return
from the giver

And then there is pain
in not receiving anything at all

No wonder why receiving
has become such a convoluted process
one that involves trying to control or reject
within a process meant to be a natural one

Let go of all the tapes playing within

and simply say "thank you" for the receiving
with nothing added, except appreciation
allowing the giver to have the opportunity
to feel good by just remembering
how good it can feel when giving to others

Channels will begin to open more clearly
to receiving
in gratitude for what has been given

Reflecting

My pen has been silent for a long time
choosing to live my life
instead of documenting it

Much has happened
many changes
many evaluations and realizations
steps towards the goal of evolving

It has been an arduous journey so far
filled with joy and fear
accomplishments
and still some struggles
The ego mind vs the higher
still clinging instead of trusting
even with all I've learned

The most important part of this journey
has been truthfulness with self
and with the Source of my being
for I cannot hide from either
any longer
and don't want to
anymore

Today, this moment I just realized
that a new journey is now beginning

I've been stuck
caught between the door of two worlds
one to let go of – the past
and one to step into – the future
by the way I experience

now
I have struggled between
feeling stuck in not moving forward
not fully clear of what holds me here

It's me of course
but not yet sure why

Reflecting, the light bulb went off this morning
seeing the old vs the new

I see the struggle
to hold on to what I know
through that of the ego mind
which holds onto such familiarity
while the one that has evolved
and wishes to trust and move forward
awaits patiently

I sat and counted my blessings this morning
to work through sadness
and then I knew
my heart was being held hostage
temporarily
until I realized it

There is a new journey awaiting
and it's really time to let go to start it
The whole journey before this
led me to this door

Many doors have appeared before
but this one is different
Perhaps there are many more doors
to come
but focus can only be on this one now

I see it as the culmination
of many seeds planted
that I nurtured and watched grow

I've completed many tasks
one of beginning to understand darkness and shadow
and one of transmuting them to light
in mind and heart

Where there are moments of clarity
seen through veils of coverings
there has been both struggle and transformation
back and forth between the two
like a pendulum
and I don't wish to go back

I want to move forward
and so I shall
because the core of my being
wants to as well

I see the inner strength
that has developed
I see the ability to persevere
to accomplish and not give up
to will self to move forward
in spite of the ego mind's fear of the unknown
or moments seeming to take steps backwards
a mind that no longer holds any illusions for me

Where do I go from here?

I look forward to finding out

Reincarnation

So you remember
who you were
Is it really
important

What is important
is who you are today

Learn the lesson
from what you remember
what you have learned
through the memory of it

Absorb it
to become more
of who you really are
NOW

Reincarnation – Remembering

I laugh and I cry
I'm low and I'm high
I run from and try
I've always asked "why"

"Who am I" said she
is "this" really me
but what do I see
I also was he

(can this really be?)

If truth be told
I am young, I am old
many lives I enfold
many ways to behold

They all brought me here
to the truths I endear
and to live with less fear
in the mantle I wear

So the answer to me
I'm not now what I see
but setting self free
and allow self to BE

Re-Something

Waking up this morning feeling low
it suddenly dawned on me
There are a lot of **RE** words out there just to name a few:

Remind	**Remember**	**Reason**
Regenerate	**Repattern**	**Respect**
Restore	**Reorganize**	**Resurrect**
Renew	**Redecorate**	**Return**
Reawaken	**Respond**	**Release**
Recall	**Restart**	**Recover**
Realize	**Repeat**	**Resolve**
Reveal	**Remain**	**Reincarnate**
Ready		

The one that struck me the most was **Remind**

With all the **Re's** in the world
it says something already exists
or once existed
and for some **Reason** or another may have to be **Re**-something
to **Remember** what apparently was forgotten
or covered up in such a way
that needs to be **Restored, Renewed, Respected**

So in **Remind**
What is actually being said
is to **Reawaken** to what already exists
taking steps to **Regenerate**
Restart in new directions
Respond in new ways
Redecorate, Repattern or **Reorganize**
in order to **Recall** and **Recover** that which still exists within

instead of being stuck in what is not wanted to
Repeat and **Remain** status quo
But to **Resurrect, Recover** and **Return** to mind
the love and light we truly are

That's one heck of a **Realization**
and now feel **Ready** to **Restart** my day
much happier than just a few moments ago

NOTE: Am left laughing after writing this because I never fully know what words are going to come through after completing what has been realized and released. This truly was a lesson for me for when I opened my eyes this morning and felt another wave of darker energy patterns and feelings begin to emerge. Apparently I needed a reminder to use the knowledge and tools given me in order to remember that these are old patterns. only coverings once again rising to the surface to be let go of, not to fall back into. And so I took action to let them go and began writing. Literally as I wrote about this experience, more Re words kept appearing as I wrote, with more appearing after walking away.

So, here I am once again being reminded that anything that needs to be released is old stuff rising to the surface to be let go of, and once done reveals more and more of what truly exists beneath it all, now ready to go about my day in a happier state of mind. While tickled by what was written here, I assure you what was being released was definitely not something comfortable I wish to repeat, and so I thankfully consider this lesson done…until the next one. Am still in awe of this process even while realizing this may be a lifetime process, yet perhaps understanding this may mean never having to reincarnate to resolve these issues then :o)

Respect

If I can't respect self
then who will respect me

If I can't be honest with self
then who will be honest with me

I can't receive from out there
if I'm not willing to give it first
from in here

Once I fill my cup
then there is plenty to give to others
from the bounty within
and then I will receive respect back
in abundance

The same holds true for anything else

Responsibility

As a child
I ran away the fist time
from taking blame and being responsible
rather than admit I made a mistake
out of childlike ignorance

The second time was a bit easier
to shun the truth
I learned to place blame elsewhere
to salve my own ego

Several times after
I became quite good at it
actually believing I was guiltless
becoming self-righteous along the way
careful to avoid making those same mistakes
and telling everyone
I couldn't, and wouldn't do such a thing
shifting blame and circumstance elsewhere
especially in things and events of my life
that didn't work well
coming up with plausible excuses that ego could live with
telling anyone who would listen
except one person -
me

The old saying
making mountains out of molehills
makes sense to me now
I ran each time from taking responsibility
and each time I did
the twinge of guilt inside
which I also chose to ignore
had magnified greatly

making the fear of being the one to blame
much more threatening

It clouded perspective
in situations with simple solutions
and instead of standing firm to find the solution simply
and take positive action immediately
sometimes it became easier to run from the situation
than face the pain of truth I felt inside

The moral of this story
which has taken lifetimes to learn
(thus far)
is that it is much easier to take responsibility
for one's actions
and surrounding circumstances that are a part of one's life
than to hide from the truth

A mistake can be corrected
and let go of
and the value of the lesson learned
can be a freeing experience

But to run from the truth
is to hide it from everyone
but self ... and you know who else

The burden it carries
will continue to grow
until one realizes
the punishment it inflicts has much outweighed
the deed

Sea of Life

I'm forming a relationship with the sea
learning to steer the ship (me)
and move with the motion of the water
getting to know the nature of it
and building a trust
that I really cannot sink far below
even if I become submerged for awhile

Sometimes I get tired
and need to moor my ship in a little quay
to reflect on my journey
maybe swim for a while
or just take a nap

And often I need to remember
to thank the sea for carrying me
sustaining and guiding me
for no matter what happens
the sea always carries me
as long as I do what I can
to flow with the waves
even through storms
so my ship will sail into the horizon
and take me wherever I need to go

Source

You sit on the sidelines
patiently
as I go about my business
learning the lessons of life
through joy and tears

You're at the edge of my awareness
quietly
with love
never judging
only Being what You are
while I'm busy being who I think I am
not yet realizing
I am but an extension of you

So I must hoe the long road
back to my beginnings
forever learning
until I've learned all that I need to
sometimes the hard way
as much as I will allow myself
until the day I finally realize
all my searching was endless activity
and all that was necessary
was to BE in the first place

Strength

When one wants to
and says
I can't
one may believe the ability doesn't exist

Perhaps there is fear to try
... because it didn't work before
An unwillingness to risk failure or humiliation ...
 ...to salve ego
Impatience to learn ...
...out of desire for immediate results
Inability to live up to high expectations
 ...in comparison to others

There are two sides to everything
If one is willing
to confront weakness or vulnerability
to take a closer look at it
and work along with it
instead of running from or hiding it
then weakness
may end up becoming
one's greatest
strength

Suicide and Resurrection

When discovering some pain experienced
carried through from another life
I began to learn there was more within my soul
than from this life alone

The door opened to my first past life memory
touching upon a life of such pain
that I ran away from it by taking my own life
for the emotional pain was unbearable
to the point of not wanting to live anymore
not even consciously exist

But apparently life doesn't work that way

At some point lessons need to be learned
issues resolved
carried on the journey into a new life until they are
with many not knowing that pain is a teacher
a road sign and indicator
leading to where issues exist until resolved

Being reborn into this life
I carried the burden of much unfinished business
old and distorted hurtful perceptions of self and others
still needing to be resolved and healed
things I did not know how to before for lack of wisdom
and came into this life to learn and discover
that I was worthy instead of putting others first
to determine my own worth and well being

From the pain carried into this life
not understood by the young child who carried it
I first learned to survive living with it
yet somehow knowing in my heart

that taking my life again would only mean more hurt and pain
so I managed to survive and pain managed to sleep here and
    there
until opportunities appeared on the horizon to heal
and perceive the truth of what had been done
offering ways to heal the inner wounds carried by my own hand

The reason why I took my life is not the issue here
Suffice to say the experience of hurt and pain
caused great suffering
feeling at the time I could not continue to live
believing the loss of someone in my life
who chose another over me
and his opinion of me
carried more gravity and importance than my life
which I in turn took away
judged and devalued it because of the pain experienced

Rejection appeared in this life
time and again
and with it the child growing up experienced self doubt
learning to place more value on the opinions and reactions of
    others
more than self had yet to learn

The pain of loss was hurtful
but not enough to repeat taking my life again
Honestly the thought came to me a time or two
but I knew deep within it was not an option
this time around
for I came into this life to heal
to learn to face what I could not before
and so I carried deep within perhaps lessons from many lives
with enough strength and perseverance to survive
until I was old enough to understand what my action had
    wrought

what I had done
and with it what I was meant to change while in this life
in learning how to face that pain
perceiving the truth of it
helped me to realize what I was meant to learn

First: That I cannot destroy a life
for it lives on and carries with it
the pain one runs from
time and again until resolved

Second: Understanding and perception
allowed me to see
why similar experiences in this life came to me
some unconsciously reminding me of that pain
being carried within the depths of my being

Third: How taking my life devalued self and diminished greatly
through the belief that the loss of the person I deeply mourned
left me with a feeling of powerlessness
feeling unworthy enough to be loved or to love
victimhood created with purpose

Fourth: That I did not have enough love or confidence in self
to stand tall and rise from the ashes
to create a new and stronger life
because I hadn't learned how
in the experience of that life

And Fifth: Most importantly
Mastering and releasing old emotions also taught me
that taking my life killed something within spirit
something I had to learn how to resurrect in what I took away
finding ways to love and respect self more
instead of giving that power away to responsive actions of others
and to determine that I was worthy of living

while discovering that life is a gift given
one meant to cherish not destroy
I've come to remember other lives as well
mirrored In experiences of this life
all which has taught me to learn to embrace life
to value self and find inner truth, strength and courage
I never consciously knew existed within
flavored with much forgiveness for self and others
for what I did not previously understand

These have been some of my lessons
taught in many ways
some harder to work with than others
yet all have left me with a deeper sense of self
and knowing in my heart that when its time to leave this life
I will no longer carry the burdens of a painful past
Instead carrying more love and happiness to shine through
as this life has been teaching me to do

Remember the story of the princess and the pea?
It's almost like that
removing mattress after mattress of hurt and discomfort
to find a tiny pea at the bottom of the pile
revealing to self the royalty of my being

NOTE: For those reading this who may be experiencing deep
hurt and pain after reading this, I sincerely hope and implore
you to seek help to find ways to heal your pain and not run from
it. While you may not feel it at the moment, beneath it all exists
love and you are worthy of both having and experiencing it.

Support Appreciation

I never put much thought to the idea of support before
except maybe when something in my life was not working
and then thought about it more

To me support was my parents
friends and family
husband
my job - -
taking life in general for granted as part of living
until issues with them appeared
not feeling supported by them

During my spirit journey
I've come to know, love and appreciate another kind of
    support
the support of Source (or for me God)
my teachers and the unseen beings of light
all of whom share their wisdom and light by guiding my way
(without judgment)
especially in those moments I need it most
even if it is I who mostly has to ask
and take the steps

Which brings me to the feet and legs - -
Now they support and carry the body
helping it to keep its balance
The arms support feeding and taking care of the body
and all of one's needs
including expressions of love

And for some support may mean a chair
artificial limbs or body parts

Then there is the stomach
the heart
and don't forget the spine
Every cell, muscle, bone, tissue, organ all support each other
making the attempt to work in harmony and unity
to support the whole

Of course, don't forget the energy and unseen force
that animates it all

Every one and every thing in life in one way or another
supports each of us in some way
contributes to the wholeness of what we are and what we do

And what about the earth
who supports us in life
in sustenance
in beauty
in countless ways

Hooray too for the atom
and every contributing part of its being
which all ultimately supports us in form, function

So the next time I think of support
I'll say "thank you and blessings to you **all** for the great job
    you're doing - -
I appreciate you're being there because I know I can't do it
    without you"

Taking Care of Now

I only know what's true for me
up to the point I've been given it
in the moment of now

What is true for me now
Is being able to see how far I've come
which gives me the impetus
to continue my journey into the future
by taking care of now

Thoughts

There are two sides to our nature
positive and negative
as has been taught
for thousands of years

Our thoughts and reactions
are what brings us
to one side
or the other

The wonderful part is
one can always
change

… hopefully
to more positive ones

Today

I'm feeling great today
my mind is clear
the sun is shining
I like people
I like me

Yesterday was different
as tomorrow may well be
There was gloom and misery
impatience with everyone and everything
including myself

But today is great
so I'm just going to enjoy it

Trust – 1

Something had always felt missing
seeming to keep me from feeling secure
inside

Keeping me feeling separate
apart from others
An inner place
always hiding and fearful of the separation
never feeling safe or secure

I always held back
from showing myself to others
until I felt sure enough that it was safe
and that I could trust out there

It became very clear to me today
that the missing element within
was trusting self

I feel like something within
has just solidified
that two parts have enmeshed
entwined

Learning to trust that inner guidance
earned that right
gratefully

Trust seems to be the glue that binds
for I am aware for the first time
of a sense of wholeness
of a true inner peace
never felt before

Trust – 2

Trust is
a companion for life
It's part of who we are
a bond and connection
between ourselves and the Infinite

To trust "I Am one with all that Is"
is to walk in truth and light
as the natural state of being

When one places trust
in something less than the Infinite
trust may appear to be lost
but can be found

For placing trust in the lower mind
and not the Infinite
is fraught with disappointed expectations
broken promises and distortions of truth

Trust is never lost
It may be covered with layers
from misplaced beliefs and illusions
trust in the lower mind that says "believe in me instead"
much like the snake in the Garden of Eden

In the meantime, the Infinite sits there waiting patiently
for one to finally realize where trust truly belongs

What a glorious feeling to find it
and not be fearful of losing it
if one's heart is in the right place

Truth Discovery

The truth be known
I'm more than one
the pieces I have left undone
They called to me
my back did turn
on all the lessons I must learn

And one by one
I'm forced to face
the truths I tried hard to erase
For what was
easy to ignore
returns much harder than before

Until I say
"I've had enough
I'm willing to confront this stuff"
and look to seek
what I must find
I will not have my peace of mind

The funny thing
this peace of mind
it's a piece of puzzle kind
and one by one
each piece does fit
unto the whole as I permit

To all the parts
that are undone
waiting to unite as one
forgive me
for I'm learning how
to gather all I did not sow

It's easier
(but not for long)
to think that I have not done wrong
until I look
at what ails me
and take responsibility

Another piece
that I've set free
again becomes much part of me
unto the whole
I yearn to meet
is the day it's all complete

Each lesson faced
to mend the rift
rewards me with a greater gift
To this day
I've yet to know
why I resist this process so

Turnaround

When one is feeling low
where self esteem is nil
look within and see
the place you want to be

For patterns do abound
and still do hang around
until one comes to see
how to set them free

The mind will keep you there
amongst the pain and fear
until you come to see
it's you that holds the key

NOT him
NOT her
NOT them
NOT there

Outside reflects in here
the pain the hurt and fear
We keep ourselves entwined
until we change our mind

It's we that holds the key
It's we who sets us free

And once you come to find
a way to change your mind
no longer will you be
encased in fallacy

I'm trying to convey
to help you find a way
to no longer have you be
stuck in your old debris

Acknowledge what you feel
that none of this is real
show yourself the way
you want to be today

Change the atmosphere
Change that which you fear

Tell your mind '**No More**'
and walk right out that door
See things differently
Create the fantasy

For once you show your mind
it cannot keep you bound
clear out the old debris
and a new way will be found

It's a tool to use you see
the way to use your key
the way to come to **Be**
the way to set you **Free**

Soon you will restore
the power that is yours
Then lift your head up high
spread your wings
and **Fly!**

Ultimate Life Lessons

- ✸ Running away does not work
- ✸ Resisting does not work
- ✸ Denouncing and ignoring does not work
- ✸ Placing blame on others does not work
- ✸ Judgments and name-calling do not work
- ✸ Holding on to upset does not work (only creates more of the same)
- ✸ Unforgiving does not work
- ✸ Ignorance (the art of ignoring) does not work
- ✸ Procrastination only prolongs it

What does work:

Letting it go, but if you find you can't, look to the following:
- ✸ Knowledge leading to wisdom
- ✸ Acknowledging and accepting the problem exists
- ✸ Taking responsibility for it
- ✸ Working with spirit and others to learn about it
- ✸ Observing hurt through detachment
- ✸ Seeking ways to resolve inner issues
- ✸ Sending love to it is always a healer (as much as can be mustered)
- ✸ Forgiving self and others (a biggie)

Who Am I?

I think I know myself
and some days
I find I don't know me at all
Something deep inside keeps calling to be heard
a shadow cast over my presence
yearning for freedom
pressing heavily in the core of my being
seeking release

Fear, depression, unhappiness skirt my emotions
seeking to be content amidst circles of joy
which are
always fleeting, illusive
never knowing why
feelings of delusion cripple the senses
from totally enjoying life
keeping me from freely loving
all that is me

I place my life before me
with honesty
Slowly echoes of life patterns emerge
shallow
without meaning, lacking purpose
rules set down before me out of all my yesterdays
collective opinion, habits formed of survival
dulling the senses
and controlling my today
reacting to words which churn memories of past
without thought to what I am feeling now
or who I am
now

Patterns fitting perfectly into the same wheel
always returning
Fears of hurting, of being hurt
fears of living, loving
experiencing the joyful moment of now
affecting giving, trusting, sharing
being
all that I am
now

Haunted by patterns of yesterday which are gone
prevent me
from totally accepting and loving those around me
without judging them
or forgiving them
for not being what I expect of them
or forgiving myself
for not being what they expect of me

As I begin to sift through all of these feelings
thankfully I'm coming to know
that these feelings are not who I truly am
now

Wisdom of Words

Sometimes things left unsaid
are harder than saying what needs to be said

and other times some things are better left unsaid

Words

Words are vibrational and powerful
whether in thought or spoken word
but not as powerful as in Being

Words in thought
seem to tie my being down
They encompass and surround
and prevent the flow of beingness
of being able to hear the wordless words
that allows freedom in which to live
move and have my being in knowingness

Words of thought or spoken expression
may be powerful but are limiting
If I think of where I am
who I am
what I am and why
then I am not being or hearing
the wordless words of I Am

Words are but a tool
a measurement of time
of space
of feelings
of thought and expression

They try to encompass expression
of the all of I Am
but I Am is limitless
all powerful
all knowing and timeless

Words cannot encompass the all of it

only create a measurement
as part of and not the whole of
the vastness of Being

Being just is

In the state of Being
any words expressed in the quietness of mind
are powerful enough to manifest quickly
far more than words verbally spoken or placed in thought

Either way
choose your words wisely

Printed in Poland
by Amazon Fulfillment
Poland Sp. z o.o., Wrocław